Class Justice

Essays on the Political Economy of American Criminal Jurisprudence

John C. Curtin
San Francisco State University

KENDALL/HUNT PUBLISHING COMPANY
4050 Westmark Drive Dubuque, Iowa 52002

ISBN 0-7872-1301-2

Printed in the United States of America
10 9 8 7 6 5 4 3 2 1

For Shay,

vox populi

Truth dictates and justice demands . . .

Contents

Author's Foreword

> **It's a floating opera, friend, fraught with curiosities, melodrama, spectacle, instruction, and entertainment, but it floats willy-nilly on the tide of my vagrant prose: you'll catch sight of it, lose it, spy it again; and it may require the best efforts of your imagination—together with some patience, if you're an average fellow—to keep track of the plot as it sails in and out of view.**

—John Barth, *The Floating Opera*
[Doubleday/Bantam: 1956, 1967] 6–7.

Two aspects of this book are central to reading it profitably, whether primarily for instruction or fun. One aspect is explicit throughout and that is the point of view referred to herein as political economy. The chances are the reader will not agree with the point of view and it is even more unlikely that the reader will find it easy going but, if one sticks with it, the chances are also good that one will find it valuable, again, whether primarily for instruction or fun.

The other aspect of the book deserves comment here because it is never touched explicitly. A distinction between preaching and teaching is crucial for this book because it is crucial for this writer. Preaching, whether to a choir or to critics, is essentially a matter of writing prescriptions, recommending policies to repair and enhance, advocating remedies, and the like. For the preacher, if not always for the parishioners, preaching is heady wine. The implication is not lost on anyone that the preacher has the answers, and is lost least of all on the preacher.

By contrast, teaching is less ambitious. Less ambition guarantees nothing in regard to humility on the part of the teacher, of course, as students the world over will attest, but the process of teaching does not carry any implication of having the answers. In teaching, what is needed is an appreciation of the questions and an abiding sense of the scope, the limits, strengths and weaknesses, of the questions. A teacher need not presume having answers at all. To be sure, it is likely that students will clamor for answers but that essentially is what makes them students. For the subject at issue, they have yet to learn that the wisdom of the piece is found in realizing what questions to ask.

A friend and colleague has expressed the importance of questions more succinctly and eloquently than I have found anywhere else.

> The human mind does not see an object or situation and then define what it has observed. Rather, it brings to any situation or object a definition and then sees what it has already defined.

Stuart Creighton Miller, *The Unwelcome Immigrant*, [University of California Press: 1968], 8.

The most productive definitions, to use Miller's term, are those which are operational, tentatively held and approached not as dogma but as best hunches. In a word, the best definitions in the sense of stimulating one's intellect and contributing genuinely to one's understanding are questions.

Knowing the questions to ask is, in turn, a reflection of perspective. A person's perspective or point of view provides the questions as a menu provides selections for dinner. If it's not on the menu, it's not available, in all probability, and if it is, one requires extensive knowledge of the inn and innkeeper. By and large, different menus refer us to different selections. It is so with perspectives.

No perspective is either value-free or unlimited in scope. What one may ask of a perspective *per se* is utility. A perspective is instrumental, as in the old chestnut to the effect that a scalpel is not better than a butter knife except depending upon circumstance. It can be important to know the limits of a perspective. One ought not to attempt an appendectomy with a butter knife. What may be asked when using a perspective is to be clear in regard to the propositions the perspective takes for granted, for in such assumptions will be sequestered the fundamental wisdom of the entire matter.

That is one of the basic problems connected with preaching. When one writes prescriptions, one has need to be certain of one's diagnoses. If the diagnosis is erroneous, the prescription can prove to be iatrogenic. In teaching, by comparison, the attempt is to elucidate the assumptions, thus, marking the limitations of a perspective, suggesting the power of the point of view by marking its weaknesses.

The essays in this book represent an attempt to teach rather than to preach. The essays which deal with the author's reminiscences from travels in Mexico and in Kenya/Tanzania are intended to convey political economy in less expository style than the bulk of the essays which deal substantively with topics associated directly with American criminal jurisprudence. Not all teaching need be exposition. Perhaps some of the best of it will inspire precisely because it is somewhat haphazard and tangential.

The fundamental point of view in the book indicates that the basic function of the criminal justice system in the United States is to warehouse a portion of the surplus population generated by the political economy. It is a perspective which accounts for individuality as an outcome more so than as a cause of human social behavior. For those reasons even more so than as a result of the vagaries in the writer's prose, the reader is likely to be offended and disturbed more often than enchanted.

For the same reasons of political economy, the perspective is indebted to Marx although it is decidedly not Marxist. Marx may be regarded accurately as having made an impact upon development of the social sciences similar to—indeed, it may be noted, contemporary with—the mark made upon biology by Darwin. Both made fundamental errors, no doubt, but both worked their respective canvasses to get clearer images of the phenomenon of development *per se*, be it biological or historical. Yet, the essays in this book take issue with several of the notions basic to Marxism, including historical inevitability, conspiracy and pejorative views of capitalism.

For the same reasons of political economy and the inclination to teach and to avoid preaching, the reader will find a degree of repetitiveness in these essays. One reason for that is that the point of view is unconventional and seems to demand more than a single hearing. Another reason is that each essay was written to stand independently of the others, thus, when it became advisable in the context of one essay to explain something it was done and it became advisable, or so it seemed to the author, to explain some of the same points in different contexts.

The author is responsible for all the errors and failed prose to be found in this book. The author asks the reader to keep in mind that the perspective advanced here as forcefully as possible is less a matter of conviction and prescription than challenge and diagnosis.

Preface

The Mountain: Matter and Metaphor

It was not the Inn itself which occasioned our interest and our anxiety but the absence of anyone who seemed to know anything about us, the pervasive presence of an array of black faces who responded to whatever sounds we made with enormous grins and nothing more, and rising straight up through and beyond the clouds, the most awesome and beautiful piece of geological real estate I have ever seen.

For three months I had been looking at pictures of Kilimanjaro, ever since my chat with Meyerhoff. During earlier safaris we had caught glimpses of it and, while in the Amboseli, we had seen Kilimanjaro from the Kenyan side rather close up and in good weather. But in Marangu, Tanzania, we were actually in the presence of majesty, indeed, we were already 4,500 feet up her spine. The late afternoon was hot and clear, and as we had noticed while Ali had been driving, the base of Kilimanjaro in the Moshi-Marangu region is wet, verdant, with soil that has the appearance of rich brown coffee and vegetation that looks like people went around constantly polishing the leaves. It is a region of pineapple and coffee plantations, now run as cooperatives by the Nyere government but which formerly were privately owned as the commercial heartland of German East Africa and, later in the century, owned by British-Dutch agribusiness conglomerates and managed by African-born Europeans. We had to remind ourselves that this lush countryside at the base of Kilimanjaro was in the final days of its dry season; in weeks, perhaps days, the rains would come and it would rain for two months. Still, it was not the mountainside but the mountain which riveted our attention. We stood in the gardens at the Marangu and shot several rolls of film as the weather near the top of Kilimanjaro changed before our eyes. At one moment a cloudless sky, the next moment a halo of white half way up, and suddenly the entire top half would be hidden from view by clouds then, just as suddenly, would appear again clearly. It was too big to be one mountain. There were two peaks of summits, an Alpine structure reaching to 16,890 feet (Mawenzi) and Kibo summit on which there were actually two peaks, Gilman's Point at 18,935 feet and Uhuru Peak at 19,340 feet. The idea that we were to climb the bloody thing beginning the next morning was no longer an abstraction. There it was and we were scared witless.

We were given a fine late lunch topped by the most delicious mangoes, we were shown our half a stone cottage in which we found two single beds each covered with a fur-lined comforter and a bathroom complete with an ancient Armitage Shanks tub, sink and toilet. We catnapped restlessly until time that evening for drinks in the bar and a light but altogether satisfying dinner, we took another stroll around the gardens telling ourselves everything would work out, and we went to bed still with no word from anyone we could understand about the climb or what was to happen in the morning. We were on our own in rural Tanzania at the base of Kilimanjaro and tired enough to sleep under our furs.

After breakfast the following morning, two young girls arrived at our cottage to check our clothing and other equipment. We were then ushered into what can only be described as an audience with an elderly Germanic woman who proceeded to describe the ascent in detail and to remind us as our attention slipped that, "All of sis vas vonce German East Afrika." Fortunately for us she knew the climb and added several vital pieces of equipment to our baggage. We were then introduced to our staff. We met two porters (whose names we never did hear), a cook whose name was Francis, an Assistant Guide named Ishdori, and an Ebo as Chief Guide, a gentleman by the name of Matei Ngaleyakivi. Matei was an impressive person but everything was pretty much a daze in the midst of our excitement as we trudged off from the Inn and began walking up the gravel road toward the entrance to the Marangu Corridor, Kilimanjaro National Park. Thus began Day One of the five day safari.

It was eleven in the morning as we walked away from the Inn. The plan was to reach Mandara Huts at 9,000 feet some ten miles away by dusk. The gravel roadbed wound up the mountain. The equatorial sun was brilliant—happily, we had been provided with sun hats at the Inn—and we enjoyed walking up as many of the residents of the village of Marangu were on their way down the road to the market in Moshi: women, mainly, occasionally walking behind a nonchalant and burdenless male but more often only women walking and chatting together in lilting Swahili, grinning at us, responding to our *"Jambo"* with *"Jambo, Jambo habari"* where upon we replied with the balance of our conversational Swahili, *"mazuri, mazuri, sana."* ("Hello." "Hello, hello how are you?' We are fine, very fine.") The women wore bright print cloths around their bodies and thong sandals on their feet. The combination of sun, gravel grade and the example of the natives taught us very quickly that we were improperly shod at least for this phase of the climb. I would have been happy to have my Addidas instead of hiking boots, but we imagined things would be quite different once we reached the end of the gravel road and entered the Park proper.

After a brief respite near the top of the road at the house of Ishdori where we met his wife and drank some tea, we reached the Park Gate at half-past one in the afternoon. It was required that we file an entry permit at the Ranger Station, a bit of bureaucratese we had obtained at the Inn on which had been recorded the names of everyone in our party, dates and times of our itinerary, and evidence that our passports were locked in the safe at the Inn and that we had paid all required fees.

Hoisting my daypack on my shoulders as we left the Ranger's Hut, I realized that the straps had already made a lasting impression. Once inside the Park we found ourselves in lush green jungle, reminiscent of the greenest and darkest sections of the rain forest near Lake Manyara but even greener and moisture-laden. I stopped in the first stream to fill the water bottle and to drink from my hand; the water was incredibly sweet. We stopped for a brief rest only once in the midst of this jungle, beside a large pool of sweet water where Matei and I had our first picture together. His presence was a strange thing. Matei was not a large man in physical terms but he gave off an aura of size and command that was beguiling. He spoke seldom even to his mates but his silence was eloquent.

After an hour and a half we left the jungle for a mountain valley of tall grass. Out in the open we could look up the mountainside ahead of us and notice the porters in the lead carrying their burlap sacks full of our gear. Their heads would appear and disappear in the tall grass and I remember thinking the entire scene was left over from Central Casting. We climbed a series of small ridges and finally Matei pointed up ahead and we could see Mandara Huts, a collection of recently built A-frames stuck to the mountainside just at the bottom of a steep wall. These huts had been designed and built with the aid of the Norwegian Government and had been open for only two years. Each hut consisted of six pallet bunks, everything made of wood and reasonably clean. Latrine facilities were something else again but we had anticipated that. Mandara boasted a Park employee on duty and the last place to purchase beer or coke on the mountain. My Kilimanjaro Lager cost nine shillings or about one dollar U.S. and was worth at least three times that much after the hot climb of the first day. Our staff served a tasty and ample evening meal in the larger main hut, complete with red and white checkered cloth for the plank table. After honey cakes and hot tea we washed in the nearby stream, visited the latrine as hurriedly as possible and snuggled into our bags in Mandara Number Seven. End of Day One as we fell asleep about nine o'clock.

After breakfast of porridge, hot tomatoes and fried eggs, honey and bread and very potent Tanzanian coffee, we departed Mandara at eight-thirty a.m. feeling very much the experienced mountaineers. We persuaded one another that we had gotten through the first day rather easily, all things considered, and our chances seemed good for a successful ascent. The weather on the morning of Day Two was warm and sunny, a repeat of the previous day. It required about four minutes beyond the huts at Mandara for our confidence to be shaken.

Our task for Day Two was to hike another ten miles, from Mandara Huts at 9,000 feet to Horombo Huts at 12,500 feet. The day's ascent began with a one hour pull straight up the wall, at the base of which the Mandara Huts are nestled. By the time we reached the top of the wall at the Maundi Crater trail we were feeling the first effects of exertion at that altitude. I can recall dropping my daypack and falling into the tall grass at the top, hoping that I would be left alone long enough to catch my breath. The grass marked the entrance to Heather Valley through which we hiked for the next four hours with twenty minutes out for a lunch along the trail. Mountain heather, for which the valley was named, were on all sides in brilliant shades of purples and reds turning to greens and yellows as we climbed higher. We were struck by the lack of any sign of wildlife; there were not even birds and few lizards, insects, rodents, and we had left the flies behind at lower elevations. The hike through Heather Valley was most pleasant and, while we knew we were climbing, we had very little sensation of an ascent. By our lunchtime respite our cockiness had returned.

I recall filling the water bottle in the mountain stream as we finished our lunch, and handing our tea mugs to Francis. As we stood up to begin walking again it was as though some signal had been given for an abrupt change in the weather. In minutes we were enveloped by mountain fog and clouds and it had turned chilly. For the first time I put on my heavy sweater and we set out on the last leg of our hike to Horombo.

By the time we reached the Horombo Huts at two in the afternoon it was raining and hailing. Ishdori rushed us into Horombo Number Fourteen, a replica of Mandara Seven, and we felt fortunate to be out of the weather as the hail began making a tatoo on the roof. Within the hour it was snowing and Carole and Jack looked at one another wondering if we had not taken a wrong turn somewhere. There is not heat inside the huts other than sleeping begs but we felt cozy as we snoozed away the afternoon. Francis brought us tea and honey cakes at four-thirty and we were served our evening meal at seven-thirty, this time straight in our hut so that we had hardly to leave our bags. The wind was blowing rather hard as it got dark and we imagined the good weather had left us for the duration of our climb.

Unlike the Park Headquarter and the Mandara Huts which have been completed, Horombo Huts are still under construction. The mountainside is littered in the manner of any construction site. There are approximately fifteen A-frames in varying stages of completion. Around these are scattered materials left from older structures torn down and materials used in the new construction. Three large old huts with corrugated sides and roofs house the laborers and, across a ravine on an opposite hillside, there are tents used by the foremen and building supervisors. The mountain stream runs through the ravine and is used as combination washing and drinking facility. Latrines are small corrugated rectangles teetering on end and every bit as uninviting as those further down at Mandara. The money and design furnished by the Norwegians will one day complement the superb mountainside site at Horombo though, in the meantime, everything seems subject to Tanzanian know-how and industriousness.

With the wind for a lullaby we fell asleep at nine-thirty, ending Day Two of the climb at 12,500 up Kilimanjaro. We slept through the night until Ishdori tapped on the door of our hut at seven in the morning, bringing us hot tea. After breakfast on Day Three we left the Horombo Huts at eight-thirty bound for that portion of the ascent known as the Saddle, a desert separating Mawenzi Peak from Kibo Summit and stretching approximately eight miles. Imagine a hammock slung between the two peaks with a steep mile climb at either end and you have a decent idea of the task for Day Three: ten miles climbing from Horombo Huts to Kibo Huts at 15,500 feet.

The Saddle is barren, nearly flat, brown dusty soil dotted by rocks and boulders of the same brownish color. There is not a tree or bush or blade of grass nor any living thing we were able to see except for a few tiny lizards. On a clear and sunny day the Saddle is miserably hot and when the mountain turns cold and wet the Saddle is freezing. Hiking across the Saddle people tend to become quiet, more thoughtful, perhaps occupied with instinctive dislike of the place for it is clearly not meant for living things. Once in the Saddle the peaks of Mawenzi and Kibo seem to surround and dwarf the climber, the wind is cut off and there is only the oppressive silence to add to the ominous character of it. As if the terrain were insufficient frustration, once in the Saddle Kibo Huts are clearly visible, their corrugated roofing glinting in the mountain sun. There is no question about direction. You set out for those huts straight on and keep walking and walking but they do not seem to get larger and you do not seem to get closer to them. There are no landmarks except the peaks and the huts, no sense of one spot along the Saddle being appreciably different from any other, no bends in the route.

The Saddle sits about 14,000 feet up Kilimanjaro. Crossing it you walk around the base of Mawenzi Peak. Mawenzi appears as a pyramid of craggy rock rising to 16,890 feet. It doesn't belong with the rest of Kilimanjaro. It is something out of the Alps or Himalayas, full of ledges and precipices, snow capped yet ugly. Mawenzi looks like an afterthought, sort of a geological haunted house. The Saddle is brown and, up ahead, Kibo Summit appears almost blue or blue-grey and white on top, but Mawenzi is black, dark, forbidding. As we got beyond the base of Mawenzi we found ourselves looking back over our shoulders as though to make certain the thing wasn't chasing us.

We had never been that high before, not while still on the ground at any rate. The last water and wood for cooking were just outside the Horombo site so that everything required for the balance of the ascent had to be packed across the Saddle. We reached the base of Kibo Summit at one-thirty in the afternoon and decided that the Kibo Huts were not a mirage after all. The next hour was spent huffing and puffing up the steep base of the summit. It was during that hour that we finally discovered what it meant to engage in physical exertion. The weather was clear and sunny yet it was brisk. I remember feeling the sweat running down my back and sides underneath my turtleneck and heavy sweater. Everyone will reach their own accommodation to the demands of climbing at that altitude. We found it most efficient to take ten to fifteen steps, rest, then ten to fifteen more and so on, each step amounting to not more than six to eight inches. My boots weighed a ton; once again I would gladly have exchanged them for my Addidas. As soon as we walked off the Saddle onto the base of Kibo Summit the ground changed under our feet from stable earth to sliding pebbles. The footing made climbing that much more demanding and slow. To try and force the pace would be disastrous but, fortunately, we were for too tired to make that mistake.

Finally we arrived at the Kibo Huts at two-thirty. What we had spent all day hiking and climbing toward turned out to be a pesthole. None of the Norwegian assistance, neither monies nor design, had as get reached the height of the Kibo Huts. There were two square shacks covered on sides and roofs with corrugated tin. Inside each shack were racks for twelve to fourteen bunks. These shacks had been used by climbers since the forties and were now filthy and well ventilated in a casual, "someone tore out a hole here" manner. But the real trouble lay not with the shacks but with what had passed for a latrine for we had no idea how long, but surely long enough so that the waste matter had long since filled the hole dug beneath the corrugated rickety structures. Climbers had stopped using the latrine at whatever time the thing had begun to overflow and, ever since, had been availing themselves of the mountainside within a few feet of the huts. The combination of shifting winds and human waste scattered about the immediate area would have made it impossible to eat or sleep, even if we had been at a lower altitude where we had any inclination toward either activity. As it was we stifled our disgust at the sight around us and got into our bags to toss sleeplessly through the afternoon and evening until Matei and Ishdori were to come for us to begin the final ascent at two a.m. the following morning.

Ishdori opened the makeshift door to our hut and brought us hot tea and a lantern at one-thirty on the morning of Day Four. We tried to drink the tea but our stomachs had taken leave of us. It was freezing, in the early morning darkness and we put on every stitch of clothing we had with us. I wore a pair of long johns, a pair of corduroys and a pair of old Bogner ski pants, thermal socks and my hiking boots, the top to the long johns, a turtleneck shirt, my heavy Irish knit sweater and my ski parka. I had a watch cap and a balaclava which covered by face and neck and I wore a pair of leather gloves and another pair of mountain mittens lined with fur. The altitude and difficult breathing, the exhaustion from the previous day and the lack of sound sleep, the early morning darkness and the anxiety about the final part of the ascent—everything combined to make it seem colder than it really was.

By two a.m. we were as ready as we were going to get and, accompanied by Matei and Ishdori, we started out for the top of Kilimanjaro. We were poorly dressed, of course, but too cold and anxious to realize it. My initial ten steps convinced me that the final climb from Kibo Huts at 15,500 feet to Gillman's and Uhuru peaks above nineteen thousand was to be unlike anything we had done during the past three days. My climbing stick was useless because the ground beneath my feet allowed no hold. It was like trying to climb a hill of marbles. The degree of the incline ranged from thirty degrees to perpendicular and the steepest portions were marked by the presence of stable rock formations which actually made them refreshing departures from the awful sliding slippery stuff all around us. The darkness seemed total. For the first time during the entire climb Matei had gotten himself in front of me to lead me up the peak and guide me along the traverse he had selected. We were entirely covered by dark clothing and, in the blackness of the

Kilimanjaro night, I had to sense Matei's presence more than actually see him ahead of me. My hands were freezing. Struggling with the footing and trying to discern Matei in the darkness ahead of me, I was also occupied with the mitten on my left hand. My walking stick I held in my right hand but the mitten on my left simply would not go on properly over my glove and I had no free fingers to manage it. The thought of taking off the mitten on my other hand would present itself in reverse. Finally I took off both gloves, stuffed them into my parka and put on only the fur mittens. The freedom of movement and the warmth began to come back into my hands at once and I suddenly realized that the incident was a metaphor which might have guided us in the manner of our overall clothing had we had sense enough to think it through in advance.

As Matei and I went on, the moon began to light our way. We had learned from the Rangers that our party would be alone on the mountain as we neared the top and the sense of possession heightened my adventure. The gravel beneath our feet had become completely unstable; the stick was simply a useless burden because there was absolutely no place to dig in. The wind was a low and constant sound and, except for the crunch of our boots and our breathing, it was the only sound in the world. Whenever I tried a deep breath it felt as though I had swallowed an ice cube. I made the mistake of taking a drink of water from the canteen as we stopped for a rest. The altitude and cold had turned the sweet mountain water taken from a stream near Horombo into near ice and, with one swallow, my throat froze.

I was down to two steps and stop. Two steps and breathe. My chest was pounding but my head, contrary to what I had been led to expect, was clear. Matei was always there in front of me, just beyond the reach of my arms but about the distance I could have reached had I held my stick straight in front of me. Matei was patient with me. He could have behaved in many different ways to discourage me from continuing and I would have heeded the slightest encouragement. I was ready to pack it in three times, as I recall, but Matei was always there, leading me up the summit, moving slowly, steadily, from switchback to switchback as we traversed Kibo.

It was nearing 5 a.m. and there was a new red orange light behind me as I climbed. The footing was worse and more difficult. I was literally gasping for breath at each step. The slope was so steep, that climbing was as though we were moving up the side of a building. I looked neither up nor from side to side and surely not below or behind, and it was with a sense of something happening behind me, something I had not the strength to turn and see, that I became aware of the dawn as the sun rose over Mawenzi.

Appearances may deceive but such deceptions are reality, too. We had been staring up at Mowenzi for three days and had escaped her haunted clutches as we moved across the Saddle the previous afternoon. All that time we had known the height of Mawenzi relative to Kibo, had known that Kibo was higher by two thousand to twenty-five hundred feet, but those numbers had been intellectual baggage.

The other reality, and the one which had intimidated us all along, had been the ugly scar, the dragon's lair that was Mawenzi. Now, as Matei worked me from switchback to switchback, patiently, slowly, we reached a point where, when I finally summoned enough strength to turn to look at the dawn, I found Mawenzi no longer above but below me. From that perspective it did not seem the same peak at all.

We were climbing now above the seventeen thousand foot level. The sun had risen to our backsides and was marvelously warming. Breathing was akin to sucking a rock. I realized, for the first time since leaving Kibo Hut, that I was sweating. Within thirty minutes my clothing had changed from barely comfortable against the cold to too warm. The larger boulders were more frequent now and, in the new light of dawn, I could see the top at Gillman's Point.

"Pole, pole, Bwana," Matei whispered, ("Slowly, slowly,") then, putting his fingers to his lips he bade me to rest, be still and listen. "Mazuri, Bwana." ("It is good.") I looked at my watch; it was 7:50 a.m. As I stopped gulping for air and the pounding noise in my chest began to subside, I was able to listen to the sound of Matei's mountain crater for the first time. It was the sound made by the wind rushing in and out of the huge crater and its caverns and snowpack, then rushing over the rim. It was a low continuous whoosh, rising and falling no more than a quarter note. Matei waited for a sign of recognition to appear on my face and, as my eyes lit up and I smiled, he whispered a one-word holy prayer, pronouncing each syllable emphatically: "Kili-man-jarooo." It was as though I was being reminded that I was a guest invited to spend a few moments of my life on the top of his world. It was like being in church. The wind served as choir for Matei's prayer.

We spent the next forty minutes getting to Gillman's Point at 18,935 feet. I have never known physical agony of the sort I experienced during those forty minutes. We climbed no more than seven or eight hundred feet and the footing improved almost with every step so that, for at least the final twenty minutes, I found myself stepping over and around boulders instead of having to climb and slide, climb and slip in the loose gravel. But even the improved footing did not help as I fought the altitude. Matei seemed at ease and not even out of breath as I continually looked past his shoulders to see the top. Each glance reminded me of "The Prologue in Heaven" where Goethe describes a wager between Mephisto and God over Faust as pawn. I thought those two high rollers were at it again, this time with me on pawn's row so that, no matter where or how often I moved, the top kept getting higher and higher. Then, unbelievably, Matei turned and touched my hand as I put my weight on my stick; "Ndio, Bwana, mazuri sana. Kwaheri." ("Yes, Sir, it is very good. Come again.") I was standing on Gillman's Point. It was 8:25 a.m. I was there. My heart pounded out the message. "I did it. I made it." Very deliberately and consciously I removed my mittens and parka and allowed myself to fall forward where I rested for a glorious five minutes. Lying there I realized I had no headache, that I had not had any all the way up and that the slight nausea I had experienced a few times was far less than similar moments spent reading my students' blue book examinations at school. The pounding in my system which I now felt was raw exhilaration and I had never before felt anything as intense.

Matei took me to the crevice on Gillman's Peak where the Guides had placed tattered white and red flags. He set and opened a wooden box about the size of a shoe box, took out an old penny ledger and handed it to me turned to the last page. The previous entry had been made by a team of twenty year old Bavarians the morning before our climb. Matei said nothing. I printed by name, the state of my residence, my age and then I signed it, following the previous entries. Matei looked it over and told me to record the date, which I did in European and East African fashion: day of the month first, followed by month and year. It was 8:40 a.m.

I got up from where I had been sitting and resting and began shooting. There was no question of what to shoot, every view was incredible, once-in-a-lifetime stuff. Shoot and wind. Shoot and wind. Matei and I took a few shots of one another, we had a cup of hot tea and a honey biscuit, and then Matei took me around the eastern rim of the crater to Uhuru, at 19,340, the highest land on the African continent.

Kibo Summit of Mountain Kilimanjaro is an enormous crater, snow laden the year round, approximately three miles in circumference. It is the rim of the crater which one sees from lower elevations which gives the table top appearance to Kili. The reality is something else, not a table top but a deep hole. Drifts of snow a hundred feet high line the base of the crater. The morning we were there the air was clear, the sky cloudless, bright sun glinting against the snow of the drifts.

Another few moments at Gillman's and Matei made his customary "Uh, huh," sound, softly, a polite whisper telling me we had stayed long enough on top and it was time to begin the descent. Our first fifty paces were what anyone coming off a peak would expect; boulders and crevices, stepping carefully so as not to lean too far downhill. Then we hit the loose shale and I watched as Matei began literally to ski down Kibo on the soles of his boots, knees almost stiff, leaning a bit uphill. I moved so fast I actually passed Matei and, as I did so, I saw that huge grin and heard him say, "Pole, pole, Bwana." I stopped at that, haying learned to take Matei's advice seriously. When I did so I realized my knees had begun to twitch. Sure that it was no more then a spasm, I began skiing and skating down again.

We would go down for a hundred yards, rest, then begin again. Each time we rested the twitching become more pronounced. For the first time now I had a sense of being more than tired, I was out of it, exhausted, spent.

It seemed as though we had hardly begun our descent when the shiny corrugated rooftops of the huts at Kibo came into view. I saw a figure in a blue parka looking up at us, then another figure emerged from one of the huts to stand and watch. In another few moments everyone was hugging in front of the huts and Matei was telling us, "Rest one half hour here, then Horombo." Ishdori brought hot tea and, by the time I had it down, it was time to gather our things and leave.

In telling this I have to remind myself that, at this point in time we had climbed the summit and skated down since 2 a.m. It was now eleven fifteen and we were just to begin passage through the rain forest to Horombo. At this remove it seems odd to me that I did not kick up a fuss, insisting that we stay longer at the Kibo Huts for rest. I did not. I did as Matei told me, and now, upon reflection, I can only guess at why. The answer I think has much to do with Matei, with the presence he had. I recall now what Mrs. Brice-Bennett had said of Matei when we had first heard his name; "Matei is truly one of God's Gentlemen. He may not know the Latin form but, on the mountain, he walks in God's footsteps."

We reached Horombo at three in the afternoon of the fourth day of our climb. Ishdori brought hot tea and honey cake and Carole and I sat on our bunks too tired almost to eat and drink. Unexpectedly, Matei stood in the open doorway, then bent forward into our little hut and put a large bowl of hot water in front of us. "Hot water. You wash."

We slept soundly following the evening meal and Ishdori called us at 6:15 the morning of the fifth day. We reached the huts at Mandara at 9:45. I swallowed a bottle of Kilimanjaro Lager and we were off again. We reached Park Headquarters at half past noon. As we walked down the gravel roadbed outside the entrance to the Park, we noticed it was Sunday, that Mass had just let out at the Catholic Church near the top of the Marangu Road. The parishioners trooped down the road alongside the two odd and tired Americans. We reached the Inn at 2:30 where the staff were their customary courteous selves, their courtesy now abetted by cries of congratulation for our success.

We slept through the dinner hour that evening but were up next morning in time to catch old Ali and his taxi ride into Moshi. From Moshi to the airport, then back to Nairobi by East African Airways and into our rooms at the Stanley. We had the first hot shower in seven days, room service brought us some food and we fell asleep for the afternoon. It was March 22nd, Kilimanjaro was behind us, and I had stood where, according to an Ebo legend, God comes to say good morning.

END

Part I

The Structure of Case Law and Perspectives on American Criminal Jurisprudence

Chapter One

Class Justice: A Materialist Analysis of Criminal Process in the United States

The law in its majestic impartiality forbids rich and poor alike to sleep under bridges, to beg in the streets and steal bread.

—Anatole France

Abstract

Sometimes, the cause of a thing can be so obvious that it becomes invisible, rather like hiding in plain sight. Looking for causes to crime and for causes of patterns in the criminal justice system in the United States, observers have been likely to see high crime rates, high rates of recidivism, large caseloads and overcrowding in all phases of the system. As observation has given way to explanation, people have imagined they have seen causes such as a lenient and overly-legalistic judiciary, inadequate police resources, a bumbling and costly penal system. More insightful observers have imagined such causes as a breakdown of the family unit, an overly permissive society, an increasing number of socially defective individuals disposed to crime either by cultural or genetic forces. Hoary great debates have ensued: crime control versus due process, champions of individualistic responsibility against liberal-minded advocates of social pressures, victims' rights or the rights of the accused, punishment and deterrence versus rehabilitation. In this all too familiar scenario, the salient reality has been hidden in plain sight all along. From colonial times to the present, the United States has been a rigorously structured class society in which differences and interactions between rich and poor have established limits and probabilities for the development of social institutions including, but by no means peculiar to, crime and the criminal justice system. Whether it be criminal justice or any other institution, several related forces have made it difficult to analyze life in the United States according to social class.

On the surface, from Lincoln Logs to Horatio Alger to Howard Roark, a pervasive ideology of individualistic equality and social mobility has informed virtually every social institution in the United States, particularly, the family, education and government. This ideological disguise has been so effective that people have imagined individualistic mobility while surrounded all their lives by the facts of social stratification; people suffer class position and lack class consciousness. For example, people learn early on in the United States that crime is caused by poor individuals too deficient in this or that supposed quality to respect the rights of others and to work hard for a living. Once learned, the path of least resistance recommends avoiding circumstances in which such a basic lesson will be challenged.

Besides, circumstances challenging to the prevalent ideology of individual autonomy and upward mobility will be few and far between, somewhat on the order of finding politicians espousing unpopular arguments. The reason is that, underneath the surface of consciousness and ideology, generating and providing direction to how people will explain life, are the actual day-to-day activities of people going about the tasks of securing the fundamental necessities of life, doing the range of things which circumstances dictate to acquire food, shelter, clothing and all the good and services of society. In these activities, day in and day out, people seldom think about the basic patterns created by this seemingly individualistic and disconnected behavior. Yet, the fact is that the aggregate of such day-to-day activities *are* the social institutions of life in the United States, and such activities occur within and according to probabilities set by class structure.

Probably, the single most powerful social institution in the United States is wage work. Whether a person is working for a wage (the higher the wage the greater the likelihood that workers will refer to it as salary and to their jobs as positions or professions), or is underemployed, unemployed or below the wage relationship altogether (the underclass), the connection between wages and buying power is a material reality central to every other dimension of life for approximately 95% of the people. The wage relationship is crucial as well to any true account of the lack of awareness on the part of the overwhelming number of those people of the fact that wage work itself is an institution peculiar to a particular and historically recent political economy and, furthermore, that approximately 5% of the people in the United States are not and never have been occupied with wage work except as a cost which must be borne, unfortunately, in order to do business at all, so that prudence requires that it be kept as low as possible. A similar cost/benefit prudence recommends that, since the criminal justice system is one means by which to warehouse and defuse the surplus poor who are both necessary and threatening to surplus value, criminal justice is a cost similar to the costs of wage labor itself and should be maintained on the cheap.

This does not mean that the criminal justice system or any other social institution in the United States is a mere instrument in the hands of the 5% at the top of the class structure. Rather, criminal justice and every other social institution is an outcome of the structural conflict between the surplus value interest of the 5% (capitalists) and the wage work interests of the 95% (labor). That structural conflict of class struggle is far more uneven than the mere numbers suggest because capitalists own far more wealth and capital-generating resources than do the 95%, not merely as comparative individuals but as social classes. Therefore, it is altogether likely that, as an outcome of class struggle, criminal justice or any other social institution will be organized and understood in ways which reflect the unevenness in wealth and in the power which wealth carries.

I. Introduction

The essential steps in criminal process in the United States may be listed as: (1) official notice of criminal activity, (2) investigation, (3) arrest, (4) charge, (5) plea, (6) disposition, (7) appeal.[1] The list flies in the face of conventional wisdom in at least two particulars, namely, that the process does not begin with a criminal act but with official notice of such an act, and the process does not include explicit reference to trial.

It is close to a complete waste of time in most U.S. cities to report the theft of a bicycle or even a motorcycle. Urban police departments often do not have the resources to pursue such reports. The thefts are real enough, to be sure, but the victims are simply out of luck. Calls to the police about such thefts may amount to pseudo-reports in that no investigation may be undertaken or even anticipated and it is quite possible that no record of the call will be kept. Insurance forms signed by police usually are no more than bureaucratic paper-shuffling after the fact. Effectively, in these instances, the criminal process does not begin to operate.

Although the incidence of unreported rapes in the United States may have declined somewhat over the past two decades, rape remains the most highly unreported crime. In those instances, the outrageous assault was real enough but criminal process as such never began to operate.

There has been no suggestion here that bicycle theft and rape are similar crimes. The point illustrated has been that criminal process in the United States begins with effective official notification rather than with a criminal act itself. Criminal process begins to operate as a primary administrative-bureaucratic system rather than as a process concerned initially with a crime itself. The distinction between an actual crime as an event and bureaucratic awareness of such an event is vital to an accurate understanding of criminal process for at least three reasons: One, the administrative-bureaucratic character of the process persists throughout as the strongest influence upon priorities. Two, the distinction lies at the core of the most prevalent and strident criticism of criminal process, namely, that the system works to protect criminals more so than to punish them. Three, the distinction is central to the most

1 As distinguishable subject matter, criminology refers to the study of the etiology or causes of criminal behavior. In U.S. universities it has been the custom to house criminology in departments of sociology, along with additional courses focusing upon criminal justice institutions separate from one another (e.g. law-enforcement, administration, penology) and to house courses on judicial institutions in departments of political science. As a new and distinct subject matter, criminal justice has become prominent during the past two decades; it refers to the study of corrections among criminal justice institutions as an integrated social system. The term "criminal process" refers to an abstract of the criminal justice system, an abstract which highlights the sequence of interrelated phases of that system.

radical indictment of criminal process, to wit, that the administrative-bureaucratic emphasis throughout criminal process disguises both the actual underlying causes of crime and the true incidence and distribution of criminal activity.

Turning to the matter of trial in criminal process, it is essential to recognize that only a small percent of judicial dispositions involve either a bench or jury trial. Estimates range for 70% to 95% of charges filed which never go to trial. When a study of the incidence of trial is confined to larger cities, the frequency will be lower; when a study is restricted to felony charges only, the frequency of trials will increase. But the important point remains that, contrary to conventional wisdom, trial on criminal charges is an uncommon event in criminal process in the United States. Far more frequently than trial, criminal charges, including misdemeanors and felonies, are disposed of through plea bargaining, a practice in which a defendant pleads guilty and foregoes trial. The court is spared the budgetary expense associated with trial and the defendant pleads guilty to a lesser charge. While the public persists in imagining that the criminal process of which they are so largely critical is one in which trial is omnipresent, the fact is that the odds against criminal charges being disposed of judicially through trial are approximately nine to one.

These two discrepancies and their interaction in criminal process—between a conventional image of a process concerned primarily with the fact of crime itself in which trial of charges is essential and the real day to day process which is primarily administrative-bureaucratic in character and in which trial is relatively infrequent—can serve as a strategic means by which to grasp the true nature and causes of the criminal justice system in the United States. In the following analysis, these discrepancies and their interaction will be used as the basic contexts in which to see the outlines of conventional wisdom regarding crime and criminal process as well as the outlines of an unconventional materialist appraisal of the criminal justice system.

II. Conventional Imagery

With publication in 1968 of a work which by now deserves the appellation "classic," Herbert Packer, Professor of Law at Stanford University, codified two distinctive paradigms of criminal process in the United States.[2] Packer's terms for these paradigms were crime control and due process. He described these two sets of values operating simultaneously as "the normative antinomy at the heart of the criminal law." Packer left no doubt that he saw these contradictory sets of values as exhausting "*the* (emphasis mine) value choices that underlie the details of the criminal process." In other words, the normative antinomy included all options and normative issues were causal factors in determining criminal process.

2 *The Limits of the Criminal Sanction*, (Stanford University Press: 1968).

Although crime control and due process operated as contradictory sets, Packer pointed out that there were some important issues in common. *Ex post facto* laws are inappropriate. The principle of equal enforcement of the law is essential to justice. The power of official investigation and prosecution of criminal activity must be limited constitutionally. Impartial, third-party adjudication of argument before the law is necessary for justice. According to Packer, these four propositions were "assumptions about criminal process that are widely shared and that may be viewed as common ground for the operation of any model of the criminal process."

Beyond normative common ground, however, Packer described crime control and due process as a contradiction between values associated with administrative efficiency and the values of judicial reliability. While he pointed out what he regarded as the causal nature of this normative conflict—"it is possible to identify two competing systems of value, the tension between which accounts for the intense activity now observable in the development of the criminal process"—Packer cautioned against ascribing either set to particular persons—"a person who subscribed to all of the values underlying one model to the exclusion of all the values underlying the other would be rightly viewed as a fanatic." Another scholar has characterized Packer's crime control model as a primary belief in the value of an orderly society whereas the due process model is a fundamental reliance upon the law itself.[3] Packer's work has been reprinted, edited, cited and characterized so often by so many for so many varied purposes that it has become difficult to select a single metaphor by which to elucidate either crime control or due process. It may be that, in all this attempt to explain what Packer had in mind, it is wisest to use the similes which Packer used. He said that crime control might be thought of as an assembly line whereas due process amounted to an obstacle course.

The assembly line metaphor describes criminal process as speedy and final. The efficiency is cost-effective. In this image of criminal process, emphasis is upon informal, non-adjudicative fact-finding, in other words, criminal investigation by police departments and offices of district attorney. The assumption is that these officials are reasonable persons with no axe to grind who have been well-trained to their tasks. Therefore, they ought to be left unfettered by legal formalities. When they file charges, there will be a high probability that the accused is guilty, so that the judicial phase of the process should be held to a minimum and stiff sentences should follow conviction.

The obstacle course metaphor is helpful in that it describe accurately the legalism of due process as well as the main objections to due process which crime control values will prompt. Due process is concerned primarily with seeing to it that the enormous power of government does not operate to punish the innocent. That is the essence of "reliability" in the context of criminal process. The value is that it is far wiser to risk letting a guilty person escape justice than it is to punish an inno-

3 George C. Cole, *The American System of Criminal Justice*, third edition, (Brooks/Cole: 1983), 25–6.

cent person. The means by which to implement that reliability lies in emphasizing formal, judicial impediments to efficiency, in other words, the value here is that efficient criminal process is unreliable criminal process. Such impediments to efficiency will involve questioning the accuracy of police work, forcing officials of government to establish a case against the accused within the restrictive canons of criminal procedure, and continuously allowing for appeal and review of both substantive and procedural aspects of a case.

Thus, an emphasis upon due process will be taken as hamstringing crime control efforts, and that understanding will be tolerably accurate. Packer has codified a contest between efficiency and reliability in criminal process as the only game in town and as the struggle which has and will determine the development of criminal process in the United States.

III. Critique

For many reasons, Packer's analysis is appealing. His normative antinomy was more discovery than invention in the sense that he gave voice to mainstream sentiment regarding criminal process in the United States. Both crime control and due process models are individualistic, voluntaristic, rationalistic, deterministic and idealistic. Since nearly everyone is a critic of criminal process and the criminal justice system, for one reason or another, it is refreshing to have an expert legal mind explain just what it is which accounts for the sad state of affairs, namely, a conflict over values. One inference would be that society might set things aright by facing up to and straightening out our priorities. That is always nice to hear because it suggests that improvement is within our reach and all we need do is look at it to grasp it, sort of an All-American "keep your eye on the ball" in a context of criminal process.

The truth is that Packer's analysis is important and valid at the same time as it is wrong. The validity in his work was that Packer saw a genuine antagonism over the means and ends of criminal process in the United States which, by the 1960s, had emerged as a feature of mainstream ideology. He recognized that historical situation and codified it in the form of his two models. That was an enormous contribution to an understanding of U.S. society as well as for an appreciation of our criminal justice system. The trouble was that Packer did not understand what he had done. He simply did not know what he was talking about. He imagined he had described causal and contradictory values in criminal process when in truth he had described accurately values which had been and remain mutually reinforcing. He imagined he was pointing out a crystallization of antagonistic values when in truth the historical situation was the development of a criminal justice system in the United States as one means of controlling surplus population and, integral to that control, the development of a confused ideology which operated to disguise social control as a legitimate effort to protect society against the criminal activity of poor individuals. Packer imagined he had outlined remediable malfunctions in an essentially sound and equitable social process when in truth he was looking at a fundamental inequity in the structure of wealth and in the nature of justice in the United States. Rather than a causal normative antinomy, what Packer studied was a criminal justice system which ran on the cheap because it was a system which helped warehouse the poor.

In explaining the common ground or consensual values in both crime control and due process, Packer failed to notice that he had idealized the entire matter. For instance, Packer cited a consensual belief in limited law enforcement without mentioning that, in thc day to day operation of criminal process, charges of extralegal police activity originating in a due process view are unlikely to be accepted as such by those against whom the allegations are levied. What a due process emphasis within the nitty gritty of a specific case will couch as prosecutorial fervor is not likely to be seen that way by the assistant district attorney. In other words, the consensus about the principle of limited law enforcement exists until actual day to day activity in criminal process begins, at which point the practice will be conflict rather than consensus. An even more glaring illustration of Packer's idealization of criminal process was his treatment of "the idea—itself a shorthand for a complex of attitudes—of equality."

Packer characterized the idea of equality as "a most powerful norm for influencing official conduct" and he defined it by citing a case at law: "Stated most starkly, the ideal of equality holds that 'there can be no equal justice where the kind of trial a man gets depends on the amount of money he has.'"[4] Packer made it clear that the ideal had become a problem for due process values because practice was often contrary, and that social class lay at the bottom of the problem: "The factual predicate underlying this assertion is that there are gross inequalities in the financial means of criminal defendants as a class, that in an adversary system of criminal justice an effective defense is largely a function of the resources that can be mustered on behalf of the accused, and that the very large proportion of criminal defendants who are, operationally speaking, 'indigent' will thus be denied an effective defense."

In all Packer's work, there may be no more revealing passage by which to show his idealization of criminal process. What he saw as a consistency problem in normative modeling is, in fact, the class-bias of criminal justice as an outcome of political economic structure. While corporate crimes cost Americans far more each year than conventional street crimes, corporate crimes have received less attention from the criminal justice system and such punishments as are handed out are usually in the form of corporate fines.[5] By contrast, upwards of 65% of felonies filed, in all jurisdictions, are filed against indigents. More than 90% of these charges are

4 *Griffin v. Illinois*, 551 U.S. 12, 19 (1956), cited in Packer, 166.
5 Marshall B. Clinard & Peter C. Yeager, *Corporate Crime* (Free Press: 1980) 112–119.

disposed of via plea bargaining[6] and the poor, both guilty and innocent, often plead guilty without adequate legal counsel.[7] The legal profession is organized to serve those who can afford to pay[8] and such glaring class-bias reflected in bail practices becomes even more so when it is understood that large insurance companies underwrite and reap corporate profits from bail bondsmen.[9] Among those incarcerated, studies have shown an overwhelming number with backgrounds of chronic unemployment and underemployment.[10] Jails and prisons punish rather than rehabilitate, as recidivism data shows clearly.[11] In short, qualitative differences in the substance and process of justice, based upon whether one is rich or poor, is a motif of the criminal justice system in the United States.

The motif is hardly surprising. Poverty is not merely the opposite of an ideal of equality; it is a material condition for not less than one-quarter of U.S. population. In the 1980 Census, the "official" poor were numbered at 29.3 million,[12] based upon an "economy line" three times the amount required for an "economy food budget" which the Social Security Administration pegged at $9,800 or less for 1983.[13] The food budget results from professional dieticians scouring best buys to provide basic nutrition, hardly a reliable guide to the poor. When official U.S. Department of Labor estimates of unemployment among the labor force are supplemented by discouraged jobless and involuntary part-time workers, unemployment figures approximate 15%.[14] The most recent studies of an underclass in the U.S. include estimates of another 10–15% of the total census underneath the unemployed.[15] The underclass is composed of surplus peoples who have no productive capacity; it includes such populations as incarcerated criminals (approximately one-half million), the elderly, the handicapped, and marginals such as migrants and the young.

At the upper end of the social order in the United States, no more than 5% of the total population own slightly more than half of the total wealth, including more than 80% of all corporate stocks.[16] Much of this wealth is non-taxable, such as income reinvested in profit-generating concerns (more than $20 billion annually), tax-exempt securities and expense accounts.[17] By 1970, the 100 largest corpora-

---

6 Abraham S. Blumberg, *Criminal Justice* (Viewpoints/Watts:1967) 29.

7 Arthur Rossett & Donald R. Cressey, "The Odyssey of Peter Randolph," *Justice by Consent* (Harper & Row: 1976) 11–33; see also, Joe R. Feagin, *Social Problems*, (Prentice-Hall: 1982), 292.

8 Leon Mayhew & Albert Reiss, "The Social Organization of Legal Contracts," *American Sociological Review, 34* (June 1969) 309ff.

9 Forest Dil, "Discretion, Exchange and Social Control: Bail Bondsmen in Criminal Courts," *Law and Society Review, 9* (Summer, 1975), 639–74.

10 Albert Szymanski, *The Capitalist State and the Politics of Class*, (Winthrop: 1978) 180.

11 Gordon Hawkins, *The Prison* (University of Chicago Press: 1976), 42–45; see also, Daniel Glazer, *The Effectiveness of Prison and Parole System* (Bobbs-Merrill: 1964).

12 U.S. Bureau of the Census, *1980 Census*, (U.S. Government Printing Office: 1980).

13 Stephen J. Rose, *Social Stratification in the U.S.*, (Social Graphics: 1983), 8.

14 Harry Braverman, *Labor and Monopoly Capital*, (Monthly Review Press: 1974), 400; see also, Phillip Green, *The Pursuit of Inequality*, (Pantheon: 1981).

15 Ken Aulette, *The Underclass*, (Random House: 1983).

16 Joan Smith, *Social Issues and the Social Order: The Contradictions of Capitalism*, (Winthrop: 1981), 26.

17 Victor Perle, "A Review of Shares of Upper Income Groups in Income and Savings," *Science and Society*, 18,

tions controlled nearly half of U.S. manufacturing assets[18] and the top 1% of Americans in wealth owned 51% of corporate stocks, 36% of all bonds and 14% of all real estate.[19] These sources of wealth are less and less available to those who do not enjoy them already, and they are worth considerably more in monetary power than is income.

What has this to do with the fabric of our lives and with problems we experience in such social systems as criminal justice? Perhaps, nearly everything. One dimension of the extraordinary power exercised by the 5% at the top of the structure of wealth in the United States is that the appearance of such people, in any capacity at all, in thc institutions of criminal process in the United States is so rare as to be statistically insignificant. There is no suggestion here that the law and other criminal justice institutions are mere instruments in the hands of a ruling class. Rather, the point here is that the law and other criminal justice institutions are historical outcomes of the conflict between classes, a conflict in which the wealthy exercise power far in excess of their number, so that a distinct class-bias exists in the substance and process of criminal justice in the United States. While particular figures will vary from study to study, there is little argument over the validity of the larger picture of U.S. society drawn from these estimates. The argument is over whether or what and how much that picture may explain. The predominant answer, from academicians, practitioners and the general public is that the structure of wealth in the United States has nothing to do with our criminal justice system. Packer's models reflect that assumption.

In the absence of any causal connection to political economy, mainstream analyses of criminal justice proceed from the assumption that the individual is the basic unit of society. The corollary is that crime is an individualistic and voluntaristic phenomenon. While supposed tough-minded conservatives espousing crime control values argue with more liberal and progressive-minded advocates of a due process emphasis over the role of society in crime rates, both sides agree that individuals are responsible for their own behavior and that justice must protect society from the inroads of criminally-minded individuals while guaranteeing the individual's legal right. That tacit agreement is the actual common ground, or a basic portion of it, between crime control and due process. That agreement is a powerful factor in the mutually reinforcing operation of Packer's supposedly contradictory sets of norms; the great debate between crime control and due process obscures the actual nature of criminal process while reinforcing an ideology of individualism. For example, consider the two discrepancies mentioned at the outset.

The criminal courts in the United States are overloaded. The particular situations of overload vary from jurisdiction to jurisdiction. In Memphis, Tennessee, criminal

---

18 *Statistical Abstracts*, 1972, 481.

19 James D. Smith & Stephen D. Franklin, "The Concentration of Personal Wealth, 1922–1969," *The American Economic Review, 64* (May 1974) 162ff.

court calendars are backed up as much as a year or more whereas, in San Francisco, California, judicial disposition by bargaining or trial must begin within sixty days of charge and this is one factor among several in the percent of cases which the Office of District Attorney will not pursue. But overload of criminal court calendars is a pervasive feature of criminal process in the United States, and that overload occurs with a mere 5 to 10% of charges disposed of through trials. Any reduction in the frequency of plea bargaining would collapse an already overcrowded criminal court system. The inability among practitioners to envision a workable alternative to plea bargaining is not because these officials lack creativity but because the system in which they live their professional lives is primarily administrative-bureaucratic; they have a day to day intimacy with the primacy of budgetary issues over ideals. In 1983 the voters of California voted three to one in favor of Proposition 8, in which there was included a demand that plea bargaining throughout the criminal justice system in that state be reduced sharply. As of this writing, no discernible decline in the frequency of plea bargaining has taken place.

Yet, according to Packer, the supposed normative conflict between crime control and due process will determine developments in criminal process. Crime control values recommend the full measure of punishment and retribution for the actual crime, while due process values suggest a primary concern for the formalities of legal procedure, even to insistence that guilty pleas ought to be declared unconstitutional because they preclude obliging the government to make its case. But the more familiar one becomes with the severely limited material resources of the criminal courts, the more likely one is to see plea bargaining as necessary. In such fashion are crime control and due process norms, as such, relegated to an ancillary role by the fundamental urgency of budgets. Over time, whatever debate may occur over crime control and due process, the ideological dialogue will reinforce and disguise the primacy of material circumstances. People are likely to continue to construe the criminal justice system as a conflict between individualistic accountability and individualistic legal rights.

One further illustration of Packer's idealization of criminal process must be included because of the attention which he paid it. Packer described the doctrine of legal guilt as central to the due process model. "According to this doctrine, a person is not to be held guilty of crime merely on a showing factually what he is said to have done. Instead, he is to be held guilty if and only if these factual determinations are made in procedurally regular fashion and by authorities acting within competences duly allocated to them. Furthermore, he is not to be held guilty, even though the factual determination is or might be adverse to him, if various rules designed to protect him and to safeguard the integrity of the process are not given effect." The rules Packer cited were jurisdiction, venue, statute of limitations, double jeopardy, and criminal responsibility. For emphasis, Packer concluded the passage with the following admonition: "None of these requirements has anything to do with the factual question of whether the person did or did not engage in the conduct that is charged as the offense against him; yet favorable answers to any of them will mean that he is legally innocent."

In sum, then, due process includes a doctrine of legal guilt whereas a crime control emphasis assumes that criminal process is about the determination of actual guilt. In the famous/infamous "Christian-burial speech" case [20] the body of a murdered ten-year old girl was declared inadmissible evidence because of the manner of police interrogation by which it was found. The accused person had confessed to the murder and had led police to the body; both the corpse and the confession were excluded and the accused was legally not guilty. How does the distinction between factual and legal guilt relate to the administrative-bureaucratic character of criminal process and to its principal means of judicial disposition?

To repeat, in the due process model the major objection to plea bargaining is that the practice effectively unplugs judicial guarantees protecting the legal rights of an individual charged with a crime. However, this objection is altogether wishful and idealized, there being no operational basis of material resources for such an alternative to current practice, and the objection is overshadowed easily by the day to day demands of efficiency. The doctrine of legal guilt will be defended by the due-process minded as a libertarian dimension of an adversary process in contrast to a reactionary, crime control emphasis upon factual guilt, punishment and retribution. That brand of debate over abstractions is just so much eyewash. The plain fact is that the administrative-bureaucratic character of criminal process and plea bargaining as its principal means of judicial disposition, rather than any abstract epistemology of evidence, provide the grounding and actual defense of legal guilt. In other words, legal guilt is less a doctrine than an administrative process. Material resources, not philosophical abstractions, mandate the institution of legal guilt at the same time as those resources recommend and legitimize an ideology of criminal process which disguises the true nature of criminal justice.

In a crime control view of criminal process, insistence upon factual guilt and criticism of legal guilt as dangerous to public safety will be accompanied by posturing over high crime rates, lenient judges and a need for greater emphasis upon punishment and retribution. The cry here will be, "Bust 'em, lock 'em up and throw away the key." Crime control values will be urged as common sense and defense of old-fashioned virtues against legal mystification and legal mumbo-jumbo. In truth, neither the administrative-bureaucratic character of criminal process as a whole nor its principal means of judicial disposition have been concerned primarily with factual guilt. Crime control values, as such, along with due process values, come under the material sway of the realities of the criminal justice system. Tough-minded district attorneys have learned to live with plea bargaining as have their counterparts in criminal defense. A harangue over the wisdom of legal guilt versus factual guilt amounts to ideological interference which makes it that much more unlikely that

---

20 *Brewer v. Williams*, 430 U.S. 387 (1977).

people will get a clear picture of criminal process and the material base from which that process has emerged.

The foregoing critique of Packer's description of crime control and due process models has begged an explanation of the criminal justice system in the United States seen from a materialist perspective.[21] In that explanation, the crucial factor in criminal process will be social class.

IV. Class-Biased Justice

Any framework, any explanation of anything, proceeds from assumptions. One thing which assumptions and illusions have in common is that the greatest assumption is the notion that one's explanation of phenomena is free of assumptions. The key assumption in a materialist explanation of human behavior is "that the way people go about producing the necessities of life—the good and services of their society—is fundamental to explaining their problems as well as the institutions which surround them."[22] The word "fundamental" in this context means causal, as in, a basis from which everything develops.

For all living organisms, the primary condition is the production of life. Without the power to produce and sustain life, people die. No mere truism, the implications of this basic fact of life are seldom considered in analyses of human institutions as, for instance, in conventional descriptions of criminal justice institutions. Throughout the whole long history of humankind, the basic means by which the necessities of life have been produced have changed and, with each of these fundamental shifts in production, there have been the distinctive markings of social organization to which we refer as epochs or eras. In the ancient world, slavery was the most pervasive means by which the necessities of life were produced. During the medieval era, production was organized around control of land. Since the waning of feudalism and the beginnings of the modern era, human social organization has been marked increasingly by the productive power of capital. For more than the past one hundred years, throughout the world, capital has been the basic means of production. Societies, cultures, nations, regions have developed around capital. Patterns of social relationships, social institutions and social values have been fashioned in response to the organization and development of capital. Rarely has any of this been self-conscious. For the most part, people have gone about their lives day to day and, in the process of their activity, have produced the necessities of life, from food to faith, commerce to ethics, industry to values—in response to the historical development of capital as the basic means of production. The history of the United States is a fine example:

21 "Materialist" can be confusing because it is associated commonly with acquisitiveness. Here, it refers to the assumption that matter is primary and causal in ordering social development and that values become more or less likely in consequence.

22 *Social Issues and the Social Order: the Contradictions of Capitalism* (Winthrop: 1981), 6.

During the colonial period, development of capital was organized by an economy of farming, shipping and commerce and, in the South, by a need for slave labor from Africa to work a plantation economy. As manufacturing increased, yeomen from the colonies and workers from Europe populated the cities to provide factory labor. The period from the beginning of the nineteenth century to the Civil War saw the early industrialization of the United States and the period from the Civil War to the turn of the century witnessed the rise of the United States to industrial prominence throughout the world. This was a process in which the accumulation and concentration of capital in the hands of a relative few was made possible by the labor of a rapidly expanding number of workers for whom labor became both contingent and necessary. The period since 1900 has been marked by the rise to dominance of large corporations within the United States and, throughout the world, the power of multi-national corporations.[23]

Implicit in the development of capital, as it was during the earlier epochs of human history since the ancient world, has been an arrangement of people into distinct yet interactive social class positions. Concentration of larger and larger sums of capital by fewer and fewer people has gone on side by side with increasing dependence upon finding jobs on the part of a growing number of people. Furthermore, at the same time as the number of people who must find work has increased, the number of jobs has declined, as current data on unemployment in the United States illustrates. What has emerged is a motif of two basic classes—the few who own capital and the many who work for wages—and an underclass of surplus population. The productive activity of those who own capital may be understood as an exchange of capital for labor which generates larger sums of capital, whereas the productive activity of those who work for wages may be understood as the exchange of their labor as a commodity for money with which they purchase other commodities.[24] Surplus populations suffer, as their essential material circumstance, the absence of any productive role or exchange.

It is essential to understand that "class" is an implicitly relational designation, that is, classes exist only in relation one to another and cannot be understood accurately in isolation. Class "is a fluency which evades analysis if we attempt to stop it dead at any given moment and anatomise its structure . . . The relationship must always be embodied in real people in a real context . . . The class experience is largely determined by the productive relations into which men are born or enter involuntarily."[25] "Class," then, is a convenient means by which to refer to the entire range of social organization emanating from antagonistically interactive patterns of production. Class refers to much more than level of income or the prestige of parents' occupation. Social class includes those factors but refers as well to values and

23 Richard Quinney, "Crime and the Development of Capitalism," *Current Perspectives on Criminal Behavior*, Abraham Blumberg (ed.) (Knopf: 1981) 56–72.

24 Joan Smith, 53–75.

25 E.P. Thompson, *The Making of the English Working Class*, (Random House: 1963), 9.

ambitions, to who people know and with whom they socialize and what they talk about. The conflict between classes results less fundamentally from any intentions of the people involved than from the material organization of society. Class is likely to provide the most accurate explanation of human behavior—beliefs as well as bank balances, what people wish for their children as well as who their parents were—because class positions and relations are outcomes of the ways in which people go about producing the necessities of life.

The logic of capital ownership is the generation of continuously larger sums of capital. The logic of labor is the generation of more and better commodities. The essential conflict between those logics arises from the fact that higher and higher wages are the means by which labor can enhance its acquisition of commodities and wage labor is a principal cost to capital ownership, a cost which logic dictates shall be kept as low as possible. Once this structural rather than individualistic or intentional conflict between ownership and labor is understood, and once the necessity of their interaction is understood, it becomes possible to appreciate the power which sets limits to social development. That power is not deterministic, in other words, it does not produce characteristics in a direct cause-to-effect sequence. Rather, the power is indeterminate, which means that the struggle between classes generates changing historical circumstances in which some patterns are more likely than others.

The foregoing excursion into rudimentary political economy has been by way of explaining why the structure of wealth in the United States must be the first object of study for an accurate understanding of our criminal justice system. A convenient way by which to refer to such an approach to criminal justice is to call it a model of "class justice," by which it is to be understood that every aspect of the system and criminal process as a whole is an historical and indeterminate consequence of the organization, administration and definition of justice along class lines which, in turn, is an historical and indeterminate consequence of the organization and development of capital as the basic means of production. Plea bargaining provides an excellent illustration.

Conventional descriptions of plea bargaining stop short of being genuine explanation in that they do not include any account of causal forces. To describe plea bargaining as a budgetary expediency is not an explanation because it begs the question of why budgetary consideration have greater weight than, for instance, crime control or due process values. Such conventional descriptions frequently involve the error of functionalism, namely, confusing cause with consequence. If tight budgets make plea bargaining or a practice very much like it so effective that officials of the criminal justice system are unable to imagine workable alternatives, why not substantially increase budgetary resources and change the principal means of judicial disposition from plea bargaining to something more in keeping with crime control and/or due process values? Why not spend enough money on criminal process so that it could be changed to a basic concern with factual guilt? Why not increase resources so that guilty pleas would be unconstitutional and trials necessary? To answer that it would cost too much to transform either of those abstractions into reality is no real answer at all because it begs the question of how much is too much and why.

By contrast with these unsatisfactory conventional descriptions, a class analysis of plea bargaining explains criminal process and its particular practices as indeterminate outcomes of class struggle. Inmates of jails and prisons, people arrested and charged with crimes, and all the officials of the criminal justice system who investigate, arrest and dispose of them, are so preponderantly members of the working class or underclass as to make argument on that point absurd. The entire criminal justice system, with plea bargaining as an excellent illustration, has been run on the cheap because criminal process in the United States is a cost which capitalists must bear in order to control the poor and, like all costs, maintenance is to be kept at a minimum. The very character of criminal process as a whole, its primary administrative-bureaucratic character, is an indirect consequence of a mandate to keep cost low while affecting security for the larger social order from the threat of those who are unemployed and those who are surplus peoples.

Diagnosing a supposed contradiction between sets of values as the cause of ills in criminal process, and continuous debate between such values as due process and crime control, is a form of critical malpractice. It serves to disguise the material reality of criminal justice, thereby helping to perpetuate class-biased inequities. What Ravitz has called "America's only working railroad,"[26] the criminal justice system in the United States operates as a cost-effective control of populations who threaten the mainstream ideology of equality and, more fundamentally, threaten the structure of wealth.

Appraising the criminal justice system from a materialist perspective includes a very different appreciation of the efficiency of criminal process than comes from either of the two conventional analyses. According to crime control values, the system is blocked from becoming truly effective by legalistic obstacles—lenient judges and bleeding-hearts who are more concerned with the legal rights of criminals than with the protection of society and the rights of victims of criminals. From a due process perspective, the system suffers from a frontier mentality of speedy punishment on the part of officials and a public who are ignorant of the complex wisdom of the law. Neither of these conventional evaluations results in high marks for criminal justice.

By contrast, when the criminal justice system in the United States is analyzed from a class perspective, criminal process earns an A+ for efficiency. Criminal process functions cost-effectively as an enclosure movement to pen and dispose of non-productive people. This is an urgent requirement of a political economy which generates an increasing number of such people. The law works as an instrument of

26 Williard Gaylin, "Judge Justin C. Ravitz," *Partial Justice*.

the inequitable distribution of wealth to classify and warehouse people who have no ability to own or work. In affecting the enclosure, the system creates a large number of jobs which working class people are only too happy to get, from judges to jailers, police to prosecutors, public defenders to parole officers to professors. All the while, the overwhelming number of people who administer the system, people who are warehoused by the system, people who are victims of crimes and society as a whole, persist in imagining that criminal process in the United States has been concerned truly with actual crime or legal rights, and that the system can be made either more efficient or more reliable or both through good intentions and rational analysis. It is hard to imagine a more effective integrated social system. A materialist appraisal of criminal justice need not involve approval of the system but it will include a realistic account of the system in all its power and brutality.

V. Closing Notes

It may be helpful to anticipate two related objections likely to be raised against class analysis of criminal process. One of these objections is that class analysis amounts to a specious economic determinism and an outdated and discredited Marxist harangue. The other objection is that class analysis is hopelessly pessimistic, holding as it does no possibility of improving the system.

To argue that social institutions are consequences of forces of production and the class relations those classes engender, is to run afoul of the prevailing wisdom in the United States. According to that convention, individuals rather than classes are the bedrock of human societies; institutions develop in consequence of individualistic activity on the part of individuals. As Packer's analysis illustrates nicely, conventional accounts of criminal justice are likely to include a basic assumption that human behavior is individualistic and voluntaristic, therefore, that criminals have chosen to lead lives of crime just as officials of the system and the general public have chosen to be law-abiding.

It is true that class analysis includes the claim that forces of production determine social development, but it is not necessarily true that the analysis is deterministic. As Raymond Williams' explanation of Marx's frequently cited passage on the causal nature of the forces of production has shown, Marx's term *bestimmen* has been misconstrued as determinism.[27] *Bestimmen* meant a process of development which was secular, not spiritual, in other words, the same basic sort of explanation which was involved in the explanation of evolution by Darwin, a contemporary of Marx.[28] Furthermore, *bestimmen* meant to set limits in development, not to cause a specific result. What Marx explained was that forces of production are the primary

27 Stephen Jay Gould, "Darwin's Delay," *Ever Since Darwin* (Norton: 1975).
28 "Base and Superstructure in Marxist Cultural Theory," *Problems in Materialism and Culture* (Verso: 1980), 31–49.

causal factors limiting development, that is, generating social arrangements in which some patterns become more unlikely than others.

The class analysis of criminal process outlined here has been in keeping with the indeterminate sense of cause as setting limits and generating probabilities. As has been shown, the administrative-bureaucratic character of criminal process, as well as its principal means of judicial disposition, are particular historical results made highly probable by social class inequities in the structure of wealth in the United States. That is a very different argument from suggesting that capitalism causes plea bargaining, deterministically, in a direct link of cause to effect.

The other objection to a class analysis to be anticipated here is related to the issue of deterministic *vs.* indeterminate cause: As long as social causation is understood deterministically, material explanations will appear pessimistic. The irony is that critics of class analysis will accuse materialists of economic determinism whereas they are themselves likely to be unconscious or uncritical advocates of direct or deterministic cause. The language of determination and even more of determinism was inherited from idealist and especially theological accounts of the world and man.[29] A further dimension to the irony is that materialists are likely to be advocates of indeterminate cause, as the present appraisal of criminal process in the United States illustrates, and, as such, are likely to understand change not merely as possible but as inevitable. But it will be the inevitability of change *per se*, of change itself, rather than of any particular change.

Change itself is an inevitable consequence of historical pressure resulting from basic contradictions and resulting human activity. For example, the contradiction between an ideology of equality and the class-biased inequities of criminal process continues to generate considerable social activity, all of which has changed the *status quo* from moment to moment, day to day. Another example is the basic contradiction between the structural necessity of capitalism to expand, which generates a range of consequences, beneficial and exploitive, including an increasing number of surplus people whose existence threatens the stability of the structure which produces them. The nature of development is that social change in response to such contradictions is inevitable and, in that process, some patterns are more likely than others on account of material forces of production.

Thought and all other forms of human behavior on the part of every person every day, occur in response to the total historical reality of everything which has occurred previously. At the moment of occurrence, behavior becomes a part of the grand historical process of development. Social change is one inevitable dimension of that development, but socio-historical change does not occur at the whim or according to the desires of any individual, however extraordinary such a person may be in intellect or prominence or what Keats called "the holiness of the heart's affections." Nor is social change dictated by organized vested interests, regardless of

29 Raymond Williams, 31.

how powerful such groups may become. There are always other people, other groups, other interests, and history is the accumulation of all these actors and factors.

Those who find class analysis pessimistic are likely to be looking for a way to impose their particular view of progress upon history. In organic developments as a whole and in human historical development, there has never been any way of doing that. People do make the future, as people have made the past, but not in any way they wish.[30]

---

30 "Men make their own history, but they do not make it just as they please; they do not make it under circumstances chosen by themselves, but under circumstance directly encountered, given and transmitted from the past. The tradition of all the dead generations weighs like a nightmare on the brain of the living."

*Marx, *The Eighteenth Brumaire of Louis Bonaparte*, in *Selected Works,* v.1, p.42.

Chapter Two

The Giraffe's Neck: Analyses of Plea Bargaining

A gun is no less coercive because an attorney is present to explain how it works.

—Anonymous

1. The dominant view is the one which the courts have taken, the U.S. Supreme Court particularly. In that view, plea bargaining reflects nothing more than and nothing distinct from nor violative of, the voluntarism which lies at the core of American criminal jurisprudence. A defendant, with effective assistance of counsel, considers the real options regarding his plea and selects among those options based upon his own enlightened self-interest and his own knowledge of the merits of the state's case against him. In that context of free give-and-take, the defendant bargains with the state regarding his plea. See *Brady v. U.S.*, *Jackson v. U.S.*, *North Carolina v. Alford, Santobello v. N.Y., et.al.* The jurisprudential norms here were established and reiterated in case law as the grounds for a valid guilty plea, *viz.*, intelligent and voluntary. See *Boykin v. Alabama*, *McCarthy v. U.S.*, both 1968.
2. One of the more critical views, *i.e.*, views critical of plea bargaining as distinct from the view by the court which has upheld the constitutionality of plea bargaining, is that the process of negotiating a guilty plea shifts the burden of criminal process or at least its formal adjudicative stage from something essentially adversarial to something primarily administrative. In this view of plea bargaining, prosecutors and defense counsel are constrained to behave more in the manner of managers of the court's efficiency than adversaries in due process.
3. A third argument is rooted in the fallacy of functionalism, an illogical doctrine by means of which results are presented as though they were causes, *e.g.*, wet pavements cause rain. While the proponents of this particular functionalist argument are unaware of the fallaciousness of their view, and are likely to dismiss any such suggestion even after they have heard it, the fact remains that what they argue is that the consequences of plea bargaining are the basic reasons for the existence and increasing frequency of the practice. In this view,

plea bargaining owes its existence and prevalence to the high case load and relatively low cost of the practice in the criminal justice system. Overwhelmingly, knowledgeable practitioners in criminal justice—judges, district attorneys, public defenders, parole and probation officers, juvenile justice authorities—have taken the position that we must have plea bargaining because any alternative is unthinkable in terms of system overload. Plea bargaining, in this view, keeps the overload within manageable levels. Accounting for the widespread and tacit acceptance of this argument requires no speculation about the intelligence or motivation on the part of the practitioners who advance it. For all its fallaciousness, the argument is prompted by the brute reality of the caseload in criminal justice, and by the intimate, day-to-day immersion in that reality on the pert of practitioners. Still, the argument is illogical. Worse, the illogic hides the actual causes of plea bargaining, not merely from the general public but from the very practitioners whose intimate knowledge of criminal process might be expected otherwise to serve as a basis for change.

4. As a succinct reiteration of the foregoing arguments, I suggest they may understood as arranged around three fundamental themes: (1) the constitutionality of plea bargaining, (2) the administrative nature of plea bargaining, and (3) the functionalist account of plea bargaining. Another prominent argument regarding plea bargaining which I have found reflected in my own review of the literature and my own interaction with scholars and practitioners as well as the general public is predicated upon retributive justice. From the promise that justice demands retribution, payment-in-kind in the form of punishment, it follows that people who take this view of plea bargaining regard the practice as unjust because it involves lesser charges and lower sentences than criminal offenses, be they actual or alleged, would have permitted otherwise. The popular view is that plea bargaining substitutes a slap on the wrist for an eye-for-an-eye justice. Those who advance this criticism of plea bargaining are not disposed toward any considerations of constitutional issues, administrative needs or efficiency, or logic. They are no more likely to agree than to disagree with any of those positions. Simply, they disregard them in favor of the fervor of their belief that high rates of criminal activity reflect in large measure a criminal justice system gone soft, a system which has become more concerned with the rights of criminals than with the rights of the victims of crime. The cure, they insist, lies in a return to the principle of punishment-in-kind for criminal activity. That prescription would involve eliminating plea bargaining altogether, and it can be written from a stance of high-minded morality and/or deterrence.

5. Yet another position on plea bargaining reflects a profound adherance to the values of due process generally and to the belief that "there can be no equal justice where the kind of trial a man gets depends on the amount of money he has." *Griffin v. Illinois* (1956). It is one thing to agree with that notion in the

abstract but it is quite another matter to find a precise mechanism by means of which to implement the abstraction, given the salient reality in the criminal justice system that, as Packer has expressed it, "there are gross inequalities in the financial means of criminal defendants as a class . . . and that the very large proportion of criminal defendants who are, operationally speaking, 'indigent' will thus be denied an effective defense." (*Limits*, 1968, 168.) In their *amicus* brief to the United States Supreme Court hearing argument in *Brewer v. Williams* (1977), the American Civil Liberties Union argued that confessions *per se* ought not to be allowed in evidence against a criminal defendant. The prominent criminal defense attorney, Alan Dershowitz, has argued for years, at least since he wrote what became the majority opinion of the U.S. Supreme Court in *Escobedo v. Illinois* (1964) while working as clerk for then-Justice Goldberg, that guilty pleas ought to be declared unconstitutional because they render moot almost every constitutional guarantee of due process in criminal proceedings. The Dershowitz proposal would eliminate plea bargaining.

Plea bargaining has developed in the United States into one of the most important institutions of criminal process. Just how important the practice has become depends largely upon one's perspective, upon the questions one raises. Plea bargaining is intriguing in addition to being more or less important because the frequency of its use continues to grow approximately in proportion to the controversy which surrounds it.

As a mechanism, plea bargaining is relatively straightforward. A defendant exchanges with the prosecution a guilty plea for a reduced charge and/or a favorable recommendation to the court. Prosecutorial discretion, at both state and federal levels, permits the latitude required to make bargaining possible. The United States Supreme Court has held consistently that what makes plea bargaining not only constitutional but probable is not prosecutorial coercion but the enlightened self-interest of defendants. There are sufficient implications in all this to occupy law students and attorneys for lifetimes but the fundamental mechanism remains relatively clear: The prosecution is immersed in a workload of criminal cases far too extensive to bring more than a small number to trial. A guilty plea is a waiver of trial. When prosecutorial discretion to charge and what to charge exactly is brought into the mix with defendants as a population who may or may not be coerced and who may or may not be capable of figuring their self-interest, the enormous frequency of plea bargaining is no longer mysterious.

More fundamental analyses of the causes of the practice remain elusive, however. Why does plea bargaining persist despite the overwhelming opposition to the practice on the part of practitioners and the public? Do we practice plea bargaining because of its consequences? Is there some underlying connection between plea bargaining and the criminal justice system *per se?*

The following analyses reflect the more prevalent arguments regarding the causes and the nature of plea bargaining, along with the view fundamental to this book, according to which plea bargaining is understood as an indirect consequence of political economy.

6. The last view of plea bargaining outlined in this memorandum is a view of political economy. Plea bargaining emerged incrementally rather than as a coherent whole which had been designed by anyone, and that incremental, inchoate development was a response to material—read, political economic conditions which pointed in the direction of a criminal justice system on the cheap. Political economy set the material limits within which social institutions developed with greater or lesser probability. Criminal justice was one of those aggregate social institutions and the probabilities were high that criminal process would function as one means of warehousing surplus population, thus, it would be maintained as a cost to be kept as low as possible. The particular institution we know today as plea bargaining emerged as the crux of our criminal justice system, thus, as one of the principal means by which to warehouse surplus people. The cost-effectiveness of plea bargaining, *i.e.*, handling a high case load at relatively low cost, is the main result of the practice rather than its cause.

A political economy based in the ownership of capital and its productivity generates surplus population as one strategy through which to keep the costs of labor low. At the same time as such surplus provides a value, it can threaten capital productivity, when the surplus grows too large, when the surplus becomes too visible and runs counter to the ideology of capitalism which insists upon individually negotiated contracts and social mobility, and when the surplus engage in activities which are counterproductive *per se, e.g.*, criminal activity. The particular history of criminal justice in the United States has issued a social institution which serves primarily to warehouse surplus people disposed by reasons of political economy to engage in crime or identified by the political economy as disposed to engage in crime.

It would appear that the frequency and the degree of reliance upon plea bargaining would increase in proportion to increase in the scale and maintenance costs of surplus population. Furthermore, in this view of plea bargaining it would appear that as political economic circumstances generate particular surplus populations not associated directly with criminal activity but threatening to capital productivity for other reasons, *e.g.*, housing, health—read, homelessness, AIDS, drugs—the power of the state to criminalize would be utilized to bring those populations within the sweep of the criminal justice system. Both predictions seem to have been corroborated by the salient facts associated with criminal justice in the United States during the final decades of the twentieth century.

- **Item.** From jurisdiction to jurisdiction, year-in-and-year-out, plea bargaining accounts for somewhere between three-fourths and nine-tenths of all dispositions in criminal law.
- **Item.** All across the United States, more than 65% of felony indictments filed are filed against indigents.
- **Item.** When misdemeanor indictments are measured, the rate of filings against indigents is greater than felony indictments against indigents, approaching 80% in some jurisdictions.
- **Inference.** Despite a lack of emphasis which borders on overlooking the topic altogether throughout the curricula of law schools in the United States, the institution of plea bargaining is the crux, the core, the nucleus of criminal process in the United States. While plea bargaining has a number of salient dimensions, its principal function in criminal process is to warehouse increasing numbers of the surplus poor, and to do so swiftly and cost-effectively. While plea bargaining is far from being the only institutionalized process reflecting class bias in criminal justice in the United States, it is the one used most frequently and the one which results in the largest numbers of surplus poor incarcerated.

The causes of plea bargaining in the United States have emerged from within limits established by political economic structure. Those limits have made it likely that our criminal justice system, as a major social institution, developed in the form of a cost necessary to the maintenance of productivity. The logic of capital suggests that costs be kept as low as possible. What makes the criminal justice system necessary is that it controls or manages a portion of the surplus population generated by the political economy as a reserve of labor helping to keep the cost of wage work as low as possible. In other words, the aggregate surplus population, including that portion of it managed by means of the criminal justice system, functions dialectically as a benefit as well as a cost. The criminal justice system itself functions dialectically as an institution which warehouses a portion of the surplus population but which, in order to serve that end, constitutes a further cost to the structure as a whole. For those reasons, *i.e.*, on account of those causes, the criminal justice system has developed as an integration of more particular institutions, one of the mainstays being plea bargaining. To be sure, plea bargaining handles a relatively high caseload at relatively low cost, but those features are results or consequences rather than causes.

What has any of this to do with the giraffe's neck? Consider the following account of that organ: Watching giraffes in their natural habitat, for instance, on the great Serengeti plain, it is noticeable that feeding patterns are confined largely to vegetation at the top of trees such as acacia and thorn-trees, and that no other creatures on the plain feed from those edibles. Of course, giraffes are capable of bending low to feed from near ground level but, in that feeding position, with its spindly legs outstretched in order to enable the creature to nibble on roots and grasses, the giraffe is vulnerable to predators. So they feed from the tops of trees. Their long neck has developed over time as a consequence of that feeding pattern, as one result of all that stretching.

What makes the foregoing account absurd, of course, is evolutionary biology and the genetic processes in which it is rooted. The truth is that the giraffe has been equipped with all the particular features of its anatomy by D.N.A. interacting with environment over eons. Being able to feed from the tops of trees is one of a legion of consequences of that development. But all that is required in order to make the absurdity palatable is ignorance of evolutionary biology as the structure of organic development.

The corresponding lesson is that all which is necessary in order to make the wet-pavements-cause-rain, functionalist account of plea bargaining appear sensible is ignorance of the historical and material structure of human social development. When, in place of an appreciation of that structure, people have a vague and inchoate sense that human societies develop according to values or individualist norms—social institutions result from a pluralist interaction of the preferences of individuals *per se*—an account of plea bargaining which holds that the consequences of the practice are its causes will make sense as well.

Materialist analysis argues that human societies develop historically, according to the following generic pattern: A productive element or force evolves by momentum and generates a system of social classes which, in turn, prompt development of social institutions within the material limits established by that force and system. To take the example of the development of human societies during the past three hundred years, the productive force of capital has generated various sets of social classes—*e.g.*, capitalist, service or home manufacture, agrarian; *e.g.*, capitalist, bourgeoisie or management, labor—in all of which the essential criterion of class position has been whether one owned capital or did not. Those who have owned capital have invested by hiring wage-workers who have produced commodities which have amounted to an increase in capital. Those who have not owned capital have exchanged their labor, in the form of wage-work, for commodities. The historical emergence of capital as the force of production in the world, together with the fundamental pattern of class relationships appropriate to that productive force, *viz.*, capital and labor, has set the material limits within which particular institutions have developed as features of particular societies at particular points in time. Plea bargaining in the United States is one instance.

What about values, ideologies, individuality? Material analysis explains values, *i.e.*, the beliefs of individuals *per se*, as among the results of developing particular social institutions. To put it differently, a materialist view pictures values, their codification more or less formally into ideologies, and the entire range of phenomena encompassed by individuality, as outcomes or consequences of social institutions. This is a view of human societies which shows people developing in terms of their productivity as a whole people, according to a pattern or structure in which beliefs and individuality are outcomes of the process rather than causes. People are seen as believing whatever they may within limits of probability set by institutions, by the regular circumstances of their daily lives as they struggle to produce. People believe in consequence of where their feet have been planted. People produce themselves.

Again, plea bargaining is one instance of this process of productivity or generativity. Materialist analysis explains what people believe about plea bargaining as among the results of the institutionalization of the practice itself. In the United States there is a fairly wide range of beliefs about plea bargaining, *e.g.*, it denies justice by denying retribution; it transforms prosecution and defense from adversarial roles into an essentially administrative role in which all officers of the court share the basic task of managing caseload; it is inherently coercive; it is within the limits of due process and constitutionality by virtue of the fact that individual defendants are free to bargain knowingly and voluntarily; it is the primary institution of criminal process by means of which a segment of the surplus poor are warehoused. Materialist analysis holds that whatever one may believe about plea bargaining is a consequence of one's exposure, directly or indirectly, to the institution itself. Plea bargaining, and the values it prompts, are among the outcomes of political economy.

At the risk of an unnecessary and deliberately contentious remark, perhaps it should be noted that a materialist analysis of plea bargaining is unlikely to win many adherents among those who approach the subject conventionally, that is, from a perspective in which values cause social development. Many people find the athletic model of the development of the giraffe's neck entirely satisfying. "See them stretching to feed. Small wonder they grow that long neck."

Chapter Three

Earthquake as Metaphor

There were heroes, villains and bystanders aplenty in the wake of the big rumble: a gentleman in a three-piece suit directing traffic in a Marina district intersection while the fire raged unchecked; hundreds of heroes, some public employees, some not, who crawled up, inside, under and around what had been the Cypress; elderly ladies who served hot food to other volunteers and to the homeless in the middle of the night and all the next day and the next; the drivers and their passengers who had gone to the Stick expecting to see Game Three and now were gridlocked; the savages who descended upon that congestion to threaten and rob carloads of people caught in parking lots and egress routes. Abetted by the media stars who covered the 8.9 through all-nighters and triple shifts, the town governments of Santa Cruz, Oakland and San Francisco did an effective job of pubic relations in hiding the looting, rioting and mayhem, while highlighting equally authentic instances of generosity, compassion and bravery.

In calling attention to the full range of human behavior on display during the aftermath of the earthouake, I intend nothing so grand as an unbiased account and surely nothing comprehensive. My ambition here is more humble. My emphasis is to explain, not to criticize or carp, on a single point only: The quake and the full range of behavior in its wake offers anyone who will look an eloquent illustration of the manner in which individuality follows and emerges from within structural continuity and change. To sharpen the point, individuality does not cause social change. Rather, individuality, for all its intrigue and importance, is a result of structural social change.

Raymond Williams, developing an initiative estabished by Antonio Gramsci, has defined the hegemonic as,

> ". . . the central, effective and dominant system of meanings and values which are not merely abstract but which are organized and lived . . . a set of meanings and values which as they are experienced in practices appear as reciprocally confirming . . . a sense of absolute because experienced reality beyond which it is very difficult for most members of the society to move, in most areas of their lives." *Problems in Materialism and Culture*, (Verso: 1980), 38.

Examples abound: our tacit recognition of the institution of wage-work and the wisdom of its attendant virtues, our no-defense-necessary insistence upon the street reasonableness of profit at the point of production, our profound notion that government operates in a neutral zone to settle disputes among other parties in society, our acceptance of poverty and the poor as among the inevitable by-products of progress.

By no means the least among these beliefs, indeed, an element in our hegemonic system of meanings and values located at one of the deepest recesses of our institutions in the United States, is our commitment to the intertwined themes of implicit contract and individualistic voluntarism. The latter consists of equal parts of individualism and voluntarism, in other words, the idea that human societies as such are collections of individuals as such whose lives are conseouences of deliberate choices selected from among unfettered alternatives. A corollary is that each person is responsible for his or her decisions since those decisions translate into actions which affect other people. The former theme holds that social organization as such amounts to a series of limited partnerships or associations designed by the members to achieve specified goals, *i.e.*, implicit contracts.

To put all this differently, Americans are highly likely to see themselves as solitary agents acting along lines of vested interests and arranging themselves with other individuals in temporary concerts which come into being, persist and conclude as vested interests merge and aims are achieved or frustrated. Some years ago, Fred Davis did a sociological study of cabdrivers and their fares in which he described the relationship as "fleeting." To borrow from Davis' work, I recommend the focus as a metaphor: Americans tend to understand themselves as individuals driving or selecting cabs and relating to others as people with whom they are associated necessarily and fleetingly until they reach their immediate destinations or have put enough money in the till.

Accordingly, Americans are unlikely to think of social change at all and, if they do, to imagine it as an aggregate consequence of individuality. Rather than consider social change as such, Americans prefer to concern themselves with endless variations on a distinction between their public and personal faces. To employ the most conventional terms, Americans enjoy their interest in the difference between those relationships which are intensely personal and loving and those relationships which are impersonal or business-like. People are likely to recognize the wisdom of getting on with it in the public areas of their lives, and limiting their relationships, but they are likely as well to insist that their private interactions are founded upon more profound and more passionate attachments. Thus, we understand ourselves as dealing with business associates but loving the members of our families.

The distinction between loving and non-loving relationships seems overgrown with more orthodoxy than analysis. If we try to get loved ones to behave as suits us, as we do for example when we convince ourselves we know what is best for someone else, how does this differ from our accepted wisdom of individualistic voluntarism and implicit contract? Especially when we love someone, are we not inclined to pull out the stops, to use our most precious and powerful resources in their behalf, as we attempt to persuade them to behave as we think fitting? Do we not behave towards loved ones as towards associates, principally on the basis of exchange or contract, in other words, what do I want from this person or for this person and what must I give in order to get it? As the novelist Trevanian put it, just what is the essential distinction in process between love and blackmail?

Then, too, perhaps it would be wise to remind ourselves of the day-to-day extent to which our lives are filled with those relationships we conventionally refer to as public. Even if the distinction between the intensely personal and the fleetingly impersonal be granted, the reality of the latter in the everyday lives of most of us makes it a topic of no little significance. If individualistic voluntarism and implicit contract operate as dual elements in a hegemonic system confined to the public dimension of our lives, the subject is fraught with complexity and import.

The interaction of these two intertwined elements of the hegemonic in our society fits elegantly within and emerges from the institutions and forces of capital production, *i.e.,* individualistic voluntarism and implicit contract are among the results of and are confirmed reciprocally by the institutions of political economic structure. In fact, that structure itself, in all its variation and continuity, is an historical phenomenon. Epochal shifts occur through historically generated increments the momentum of which gives rise to appropriate institutions of class and belief which, in turn, are superseded by successive generations of material forces and resulting institutions. The process of history is social evolution, but that is seldom the manner in which Americans approach or understand any of it.

While the hegemonic system which includes individualistic voluntarism and implicit contract is a consequence of historically generated shifts, metaphorically, with about the same relationship to individuality as geological strata and fault lines, these beliefs tell a different story. As we sit around our council fires, our folklore of individualistic voluntarism and implicit contract tell us that wet pavements cause rain, and that heroism and savagery are characteristics of individuals which cause earthquakes.

Functionalism is a doctrinal fallacy according to which results are presented as though they were causes. People are likely to recognize the fallacy as such only so long as examples are confined to commonplace abstractions, such as the notion that wet pavements cause rain or that individuality causes earthquakes. As soon as illustrations move to something material about which people are likely to be informed by folklore, the fallacy as such is likely to go unrecognized. Consider the following instances of functionalism:

1. As a practice in the criminal justice system in the United States, plea bargaining accounts for upwards of 75% of all criminal dispositions. This practice results from a combination of scarce resources and high caseload.
2. The white-faced or Masai giraffe in the Serengeti plain of East Africa feed largely on vegetation at the tops of the thorn trees which proliferate in that region. The species developed its elongated neck in consequence of that feeding pattern.

3. People send their children to school in the United States because, among other factors, they are concerned about education and the well-being of their offspring.
4. Industriousness and schedule-integrity, as personal characteristics of individuals, generate highly productive social systems both in public and business sectors. Since a higher percentage of persons in Japan are more industrious and more concerned with maintaining schedules than in the United States, Japan is more productive than the United States.
5. History results from the decisions and actions of exceptional individuals who inspire and lead less exceptional individuals along lines of concerted activities.
6. Evolution is a process caused by individual organisms attempting to cope successfully with environmental demands.

How many of these statements did you recognize as fallacious on the grounds that they confused what were in fact results with causes? Actually, each and all of the statements illustrate functionalism.

The practice in the United States in our criminal justice system which we refer to as plea bargaining in fact serves a high caseload at relatively low costs. This is a matter of fact, as any comparison of plea bargaining with the alternative of trial will demonstrate, but the practice is one result of the material forces which generate the caseload and the concern for keeping costs low, especially in the public sector and even more particularly in the criminal process.

The Masai Giraffe in fact feeds largely from the tops of trees throughout the Serengeti. The stance in which a giraffe can feed from ground level is precarious and makes them more easy prey for predators, but the long neck of the Masai and other species of giraffe has been caused by evolutionary forces and its feeding pattern is one result of those forces.

People in the United States are pleased to send their kids to schools in consequence of the institution of compulsory education. Whatever the nature or extent of actual concern for education people may possess as individuals or in distinguishable family groups is a result of that institution which, in turn, has been a result of other institutions generated and arranged historically.

In industrial economies, people are likely to be encouraged to prize and practice industriousness and schedule-integrity among other means of maintaining the political economic structure which, in turn, generates the productivity. The political economic circumstance of the United States in the wake of World War II made a U.S.-sponsored recovery of Japan at first possible, then probable, then a fact. Alongside a host of other factors, that recovery in state of the art structure generated high productivity. The highly productive political economic structure in Japan has engendered widespread industriousness and schedule-integrity among Japanese workers, and these characteristics had been implicit for generations in traditional Japanese culture. For example, some of the same historically generated qualities of temperament which resulted from such institutions as reverence for the elderly and the family also made it likely that the majority of Japanese would revere the emperor and obey officials in the government as they marched dutifully to war, then to defeat.

History encompasses lives which turn out to have been extraordinary, largely or in some particular moment, alongside people whose lives turn out to have been what people will think of as ordinary. These differences are among the results of institutional patterns historically generated. At birth, it was likely that Winston Spencer Churchill would lead a life more noteworthy than many of his contemporaries and, in fact, that turned out to have been the case. Buck Helm was unknown except to family, friends he had made along the Oakland waterfront as a dockworker and his home town of Weaverville. Then he was found still alive under the Cypress and his life became extraordinary. Helm was both tough enough to have survived and fortunate enough not to have been crushed, but his individuality did not generate his fame any more than it caused the freeway to pancake.

Evolution is a process featuring a combination of continuity and variation. Evolution also is a theoretical explanation of the process by which living organisms develop. In the absence of an alternate theory which makes more precise sense of more data, evolution is a theory without which all that we know about the biological sciences would make no sense. The process of evolution is generated and proceeds by the interaction of sets of DNA molecules arranged in patterns, to which we refer as species, families and genera, interacting with the more particular demands of habitat along a range of more or less stable environments. Equipped and prompted by DNA, organisms struggle to live, to live and survive, to survive and procreate. The struggle occurs on the part of populations of organisms and becomes more or less successful at the same level. Some populations are successful in a particular environment while others are not, but the death of an organism is hardly the same as the extermination of a population or the extinction of a species. Coping is the motif with relative success or failure as the statement of fitness, but the causal material forces are DNA and environmental interaction, with talent and fitness as consequences.

At whatever order of generality we may consider appropriate, be it at the level of some specific instance such as the neck of the giraffe or the practice of plea bargaining in the U.S. system of criminal justice, or at a somewhat higher level of generality such as the rise of values regarding education or values consistent with industrial productivity, or at an even higher level of generality such as history and evolution *per se*, the same point can be reiterated: Structure is the source of authentic individuality. Historically generated material phenomena make some results more likely than other results. The institutions of a society inform people about what is possible, what is appropriate, what is ludicrous, what is criminal. The information is packaged from fashion to child care to heroism and savagery. The institutions result from historical momentum, less from individualistic choices or designs, and those institutions order probabilities across entire societies, not individualistically by voluntarism and contract but socially by historical momentum and evolutionary struggle. Some do, others don't.

Just that enormously interesting and significant difference, between those who do and those who don't, is a consequence rather than a cause of social change. Individuality is another name for that intriguing and important difference, and it emerges from historically generated social structures, rather like people responding to an earthquake.

The Red Dust at Tsavo

On each of the five mornings after I had come down from Kilimanjaro and had flown first to Nairobi and then to the coastal village of Malindi, I had been aware of awakening just before dawn, as the first light appeared on the Indian Ocean horizon. On each of these mornings I had made a cup of Kenyan coffee, taken my cup onto the small balcony which connected my room at the Sinbad with the beach, and sat there to watch the orange ball rise out of the ocean. This morning, my last dawn in Malindi, at least for this trip, I was doing the same thing, sipping the rich coffee, watching the dawn and reflecting on my experiences in East Africa. On this last morning I suppose it was natural enough that my thoughts were on Malindi.

I was aware of the change in attitude regarding this place. My arrival had been a combination of anticipating the pleasures of relaxation after the rigors of the mountain and an immediate sense of the incredibly lush beauty of Malindi, everything growing in vivid hues and, just as the jungle gave way to the ocean, a pervasive whiteness, nearly blinding in the sunshine, from the endless beach to the stucco of the hotels alongside the curved bay. The days I had spent in Malindi had fulfilled the promise of my arrival, yet, here I was on the morning of departure, without so much as a trace of sadness or regret over the immediate prospect of leaving paradise.

There was no doubt in my mind that the sun, sand, surf, accomodations and amenities make Malindi a paradise of sorts. It had been that paradise which had greeted my eyes on arrival and had occasioned in me thoughts of wanting to remain there forever. As a paying guest at the Sinbad, life had been sweet, and I had no reason to suppose that, had I stayed at one of the other beachfront hotels along the bay—the Marlin, Lawford's—anything would have been less pleasant.

Three fine meals a day, tea and delicious honey cakes at four every afternoon, luxurious appointments even to air conditioning, the beach for strolling and running, the ocean surf, the hotel pool and bar where one can get a dozen Indian Ocean oysters and a Pimm's cup for about twenty-five cents U.S. money. Yet, there had been some part of me, some region of myself deeper in my innards than I know, which all along had told me that all was not well in Malindi, that Malindi was a flawed paradise at best.

I was not sure just what bothered me. I knew it was no aversion to decadence nor any sense that I should have been spending my days in more significant pursuits. Was it as simple as some compulsion to invent a flaw in an otherwise perfect stone? Perhaps, though I knew that was not the entire answer and I didn't imagine it was even the larger part of the answer. As I sat watching the dawn over an immense and calm ocean, I realized that the only sour notes during my stay in Malindi had been sounded not by the place but during my interactions with my fellow tourists.

Most of the other guests at the Sinbad, as well as the other hotels, were from the U.K. In conversation with these people and in snatches of conversations among them which some particular circumstance made it next to impossible for me not to overhear, I had discerned a predominant attitude on their part toward Malindi, and that was the source of my upset. I had reminded myself that the attitude of the Britisher was complicated by two pieces of structural reality or, if you will, by history. One of these pieces was an act of imagination, the other geography.

What has been described so often by so many as the arrogance of the English may be a bit easier to appreciate in certain regions of the earth than in others and I think East Africa is one of those places. In the British imagination, Kenya still belongs to them; it remains a part of the Empire. Their imagination works in a fashion similar to a situation in which one is learning a second language and, despite increasing vocabulary and syntactic facility, continues to think in one's native tongue. The British know better but that doesn't alter their attitude.

Geographically, the Kenyan coast is to the U.K. what Hawaii is to Americans and Canadians who live in the western section of their countries. It is easy to leave Heathrow in a British Airways jumbo, connect with an East African Airways "Fokker Friendship" at Nairobi and, in twelve to thirteen hours all told, one can be poolside in Malindi. Time and charges are well within the reach of the upper middle class in the U.K. and Malindi makes a fine spot for honeymooning as well as for more relaxed and staid vacations.

Recognizing these complications in the attitude of the Britisher did not relieve my anxiety, though it did allow me to appreciate that what I was disturbed about was far from a simple thing. However, as I sat and thought about it I decided the matter could be put simply: In a nutshell it was that Malindi was in Africa and that the tourists with whom I had chatted will return to old Graymere to say that they have been in Africa. In fact, they will have been there. In truth, they will not have been there. That was it, that was the source of my discomfort. Malindi had been something less than paradise for me on account of a discrepancy between fact and truth.

As I sat there, thinking this through, it occurred to me that it was downright silly for me to presume the slightest degree of proprietary responsibility or identification with East Africa. No attitude would be a more perfect example of the instant expert. After a few months in Kenya and Tanzania, there I sat looking at the Indian Ocean and feeling superior to people who decided to spend a week or two in *La Dolce Vita* Malindi. Outrageous, silly, presumptuous, yet, there it was, That was precisely how I felt.

They had been to East Africa but had not seen Tsavo and the red elephants. They had not seen the green hills of Ngorongoro nor the Masai shepherding their cattle on the slopes of Olmuti. They had been to Africa and had seen no Kikuyu woodcarvers, no Kikuyu women carrying the family produce to market atop their heads. They had not heard Masai warriors in the Amboseli sing of the rhino. They had not seen the Seregeti with its abundant herds, packs, troops and prides. They had seen neither giraffe nor cheetah. They had been to Africa but had not talked with Kenyon policemen nor joked with a Luo cabdriver in Nairobi about the prolific baby-producing capacities of the Kikuyu. They had not seen the great cats make a kill, then guard it from vultures and hyena. They had not seen hippo bathe in the muddy waters of the Ngorongoro Crater. They had been to East Africa but had not visited Olduvai, had not talked to Dr. Mary nor visited her son Richard at the Lake Rudolph dig. They had seen neither Lake Victoria nor the Great Rift Valley. They had not walked amid the smells, sights and sounds of the marketplace in Arusha; they had not bargained with Tanzanian merchants for cloth, carvings and batiks. They had not had so much as a glimpse of Kilimanjaro. They had not stood in the Amboseli watching the elephants cool themselves in the waterhole with Kibo and Mawenzi peaks in the background, the whole mountain ringed with white clouds at fifteen thousand and capped with clear blue skies and sunshine from sixteen thousand up. They had not stood on Gillman's or Uhuru with Africa at their feet, nor were they even aware of not haying done any of these things, but they had been to Africa.

I realized I resented their physical and intellectual sluggishness. I did not enjoy the realization that fine people who speak English admirably suffer from imaginations so impoverished as to consider Africa only in terms of the sweet life in Malindi. They had not earned it.

I did not think it necessary that these others should do what I had done but I was convinced that they should have done something more than transport themselves from the Commonwealth Club in London to Pool Bar at the Sinbad. What was required, I thought, was that visitors to East Africa make a deliberate effort to experience the place in terms, sights and sounds as near to those of the Kenyan or Tanzanian resident as possible. The visitor cannot *become* an East African, of course, but it was the deliberate attempt at empathy which was important.

In East Africa that attempt will be uncomfortable and inconvenient and frustrating at least as often as it will prove pleasant. But there can be no substitute for having been in a place, tasted and touched it. Tsavo is a hot, dry and dusty hell of a place most of the year but, coughing on the red dust and blowing it out of my nostrils, I knew where I was and, when I had left Tsayo, I knew something, if only a little, of where I had been. Struggling to see in the swirling red dust, I understood perhaps one half degree more keenly why the elephants there were red and why they walked such distances to cool themselves in whatever mud they might find. These lords of Tsavo, and all the creatures and peoples of East Africa struggling to survive, have my respect. I cannot say I respected my fellow guests at Malindi. They had not struggled. They bathed at will in cool water without having walked through red dust.

Part II

Law Enforcement and the Courts on Search and Seizure

Chapter 4

The Presumption of Innocence: Normative and Constitutional Considerations

"The presumption of innocence is a direction to officials about how they are to proceed, not a prediction of outcome. The presumption of guilt, however, is purely and simply a prediction of outcome."

—Herbert Packer,
The Limits of the Criminal Sanction,
(Stanford University Press: 1968), 161.

"No person . . . shall be compelled in any criminal case to be a witness against himself, nor be deprived of life, liberty, or property, without due process of law . . ."(Fifth Amendment)

". . . nor shall any State deprive any person of life, liberty, or property, without due process of law . . ." (Fourteenth Amendment)

—*The Constitution of the United States*

1. A Story of Three Umpires

Three umpires had worked a game on a humid and dusty afternoon. The game had been won by a score of three-to-two and everything had been close throughout the nine innings. The umps were in the clubhouse relaxing, having a beer, and they began to comment on how each of them had made close calls.

The first umpire to deliver an opinion about the generic quality in his close calls said, "There's only one right way to call a game. I calls 'em the way they are."

A second opinion was heard from: "Yeah, well I think you miss the point 'cause you call games the same way I do and I calls 'em the way I sees 'em."

The last of the three umps to offer a point of view was a man customarily given to being taciturn. Accordingly, he had stayed silent during most of the conversation that afternoon but now he spoke his mind, succinctly: "They ain't nothin' 'till I calls 'em."

Some stories do not require and may be impaired by analysis. They have a quality of the sort Steinbeck had in mind when he wrote of Ed "Doc" Ricketts that a truly great scientist could explain his work to a child. The salient lessons taken from such stories are significant and clear as crystal the moment we hear or read them.

The story of the three umpires is not one of those. The lessons to be had by reflecting upon the umpires' conversation are valuable ones but they are as well points of view about the nature of things which beg amplification and explanation. In a word, the lessons are aporetic. In the interests of clarity more than consensus, those lessons demand analysis.

2. The First Umpire

"There's only one right way to call a game. I calls 'em the way they are."

The founder of the German school of historiography, Leopold von Ranke, was of a similar opinion regarding the nature of his craft. His intention was to write history as it actually had happened. Nineteenth-century German historiography is a deliberately obscure and esoteric analogy: In order to see the analogy at all, considerable effort must be expended and, in the process, the deeper lessons to be learned from the first umpire may be clarified.

To write history actually as it happened is an ambitious aim. Some would call it presumptuous. The presumptuousness lies in an assumption, as presumptuousness often does, that some means are available to the historian's intellect by virtue of which he can recreate the past, not in his own image or according to any set of issues or agenda which his own time and place recommend, but strictly in accordance with past reality.

The view of reality and human intellect reflected in Herbert Packer's model of criminal process to which he referred as "crime control" shares with nineteenth-century German historiography and with the first umpire a basic assumption, *viz.*, that by some force of training, rigor and dedication it is reasonable to imagine that a portion or the whole of the past can be recreated as it actually took place. The umpire was speaking of the most recent nine innings he had worked, and of all the games before that. The police officer, the prosecutor, the citizen who advocate the norms of crime control as imperatives will have reference to some criminal activity which has occurred. Von Ranke and advocates of his school of historiography had in mind history as a whole. However, for all the variation in topic and scope of inquiry, one common denominator was the basic assumption that their insistence upon recreating reality made sense.

3. A Distinction, Accompanied by an Apology

With apologies to the Jesuits who have made a living for centuries, in part by means of a process of teaching and learning which rests upon positing a point of view and then offering a series of distinctions so that the entire lesson is didactic and complex, the salient lessons to be had by reflecting upon what the first umpire had to say beg a distinction: Is the meaning of the basic assumption a matter of actual accomplishment or is it, rather, a process in which one strives to move closer and closer to the ideal but never actually to achieve it? Is the great truth poetic or scientific?

To be sure, if one understands von Ranke to have claimed nothing more than to aim toward approximating past reality as closely as the human intellect permits, nineteenth-century German historiography becomes more ambitious than presumptuous. If police officers who insist that their informal, non-adjudicative procedures are both efficient and reliable in screening suspects so that, when an investigation has been completed, the truly important dimension of criminal process has been completed as well and all that ought to be required from that point on is a form of rubber-stamping of police work by the courts, are understood to have claimed nothing more than that they are trained and dedicated professionals striving industriously toward the ideals of fact-finding, then to be sure, crime control values regarding criminal process are not likely to engender much opposition. When the first umpire said there was only one righteous procedure and that was to say it like it is, if he is taken to have meant only that calling close plays ought to be rooted in empirical circumstances and ought to be free of prejudice or vested interests, the likelihood is that the other umps that afternoon would have nodded their heads in agreement. The more fundamental question is whether and to what extent the ambitious-but-less-presumptuous interpretation most accurately reflects the separate contexts.

How reasonable is it to imagine that the first umpire had never thought about the generic process in which calls were made prior to his conversation with his colleagues on the afternoon of the story? How reasonable is it to imagine that the first umpire was oblivious to versions of that process other than his own? On the other hand, how reasonable is it to imagine that the first umpire had fashioned his explanation incrementally over time, that he had put it together bit-by-bit as he reflected about the game and as he developed an overall sense of how and where the game fit in larger schemes? It is arguable, at least, that when the first umpire rendered his judgment he did so in expectation of being understood to have taken one position among alternatives.

The historical record which includes development of the German school of historiography in the nineteenth century leaves very little reasonable doubt that von Ranke was aware of alternate approaches to the writing of history and eager to clarify his particular perspective. His eagerness may have stemmed from an array of factors but they surely included a notion fiercely held that the Germanic, so-called "scientific" school was predicated upon an approach to the writing of history which was superior, both as regards intent and actual productivity, to any and all alternate analyses.

When police officers argue against what they see as undue supervision by the judiciary and attorneys of law enforcement procedures and conclusions, it is unlikely that those peace officers have direct knowledge of or are capable of articulating any formal models, maps or perspectives regarding criminal process, whether those models mirror their own views or reflect alternate explanations. But that is a reflection of the pervasively low quality of formal education on the part of police officers rather than a warrant for concluding that cops do not have an abiding sense of the distinctiveness and urgency of their own ways of thinking about the world. Based on every scrap of data available, no single generalization is more patent and compelling than that police have a profound sense of the distinctive superiority of their approach to criminal process—in comparison to all other approaches.

Therefore, the salient lesson offered by the first umpire is not only about ambition but about presumption. Indeed, the lesson deals with a particular presumption which, in contexts as varied as police work and nineteenth-century German historiography, will be presented as no more than the simple truth, namely, that the past is available to the human mind for re-creation in fact.

The salient implications of this presumption for historiography are not within the scope of this writing, but the implications for police work as a dimension of criminal process in the United States are important to the present focus on the presumption of innocence in American jurisprudence. What Herbert Packer has termed "the presumption of guilt" in a context of the crime control perspective on criminal process cannot be appreciated entirely apart from the deeper presumption regarding epistemology, nor can the essential distinction between presumed guilt and presumed innocence be understood accurately. Unless the latter distinction is grasped, it is not possible to take hold of due process itself, in either of the contexts in which it has significance, *viz.*, as a fundamental norm of American law and as a profound feature of the *Constitution of the United States*.

All of this is complicated enough and, if the subject is tackled when one is not equipped with a working knowledge of the historical development of Anglo-American jurisprudence, complexity can be transformed quickly into incoherence. Therefore, it seems prudent to move slowly by making a single point only, prior to considering what the second umpire had to offer. The point is that the presumption of guilt is a normative prediction of outcome in a particular context based upon a more profound presumption that the past relevant to the particular has been re-created in fact, therefore, justice demands punishment for the crime and any other judicial outcome will amount to justice denied. The essence is a focus upon the past as basis for predicting what ought to occur in the future, *i.e.*, a focus upon outcome which presumes a knowledge of the past in fact.

4. The Second Umpire and *The Heavenly City*

Carl Lotus Becker is an intriguing figure in American historiography. Becker authored a number of highly significant works, each of which he approached from the generic historiographical perspective which has come to be known as "historical relativism." Whether writing on historiography itself, as in *Detachment and the Writing of History,* or on the Declaration of Independence in a work bearing that title, or on the *philosophes* and eighteenth-century European intellectual tradition, as in *The Heavenly City of the Eighteenth-Century Philosophers*, Becker's lively and lucid historical prose was an expression of the author's fundamental belief that history was to be written most valuably from a perspective made manifest to the historian in his analysis of the salient issues of his time. Thus, the American Declaration of Independence was analyzed by Becker and addressed to an audience of the citizenry of the twentieth century on account of their need to appreciate the wisdom and urgency of the unity of a whole people. Becker thought of von Ranke and other exponents of the German school as exemplars of ambition and presumption run riot. It was nonsense, Becker was convinced, to imagine that the past was available to the human intellect for re-creation in fact. Rather, Becker held, the past was available for imaginative editing based upon perceived editorial policy.

Becker would have included the first umpire in the same population as van Ranke and the so-called "scientific" historians. Among the umpires, Becker would have favored the second gentleman's view of how the game was called. "I calls 'em the way I sees 'em" is a vulgar expression of what Becker's more esoteric view of historiography was about. Whether as vulgarity or scholarship, the common denominator was a sense of a distinction in kind between reality and perception, combined with an abiding awareness of the limitations imposed by the distinction upon perception.

The epistemology or theory of knowledge underlying the second umpire's view of things frequently is misunderstood as arrogance stemming from discretionary authority. The error is to misunderstand "I calls 'em the way I sees 'em" as though the umpire had said, "I calls 'em any way I want 'em."

For example, in a context of constitutional process in the United States, the fundamental evaluation of what has come to be known as "judicial activism" on the part of those who profess what has come to be known as "judicial conservatism" reflects two generic mistakes: (1) Conservatives imagine substantive due process and an emphasis upon penumbral rights to be relativism, a jurisprudential version of Becker's historiography when, in fact, fairness doctrines based in Fifth and Fourteenth Amendment clauses, as well as an inclination to find implications in what the *Constitution* makes explicit, reflect a view of things more closely represented by the third umpire than by the second. (2) Conservatives imagine relativism, over and above questions of its relevance, as an arbitrary misuse of authority, rather than as an arguable epistemology based upon a distinction in kind between reality and perception.

Despite the occasional eloquence and consistent clarity of judicial activists from Brandeis and Cardozo and Frankfurter through Warren and Douglas to Brennan and Marshall, despite holdings in *Palko v. Connecticut* (1937), *Wolf v. Colorado* (1949), *Griswold v. Connecticut* (1954), and *Mapp v. Ohio* (1961), judicial conservatives from John Marshall Harlan through Byron White and Warren Burger to William Rehnquist and at least four and arguably as many as seven of his colleagues on the current Court have insisted vehemently that substantive due process and a tendency toward finding constitutional implications between the lines as it were of the supreme law of the land places judges at large, on horseback, so to speak. When the senior U.S. Senator from Massachusetts entrapped Robert Bork into answering the question of whether in the judge's view the *Constitution* encompassed a fundamental right to privacy, Bork's nomination to the Court was dead. Kennedy knew that Bork, as an articulate advocate of judicial conservatism, was compelled to see the penumbra of privacy as a doctrine stemming more from activist justices than from the *Constitution.*

5. The Third Umpire and Due Process

To reiterate, it is an error, whether committed by judicial conservatives inveighing against judicial activism or in any context, to construe substantive due process as relativism. It is an error to do so even when relativism is appreciated accurately as an epistemology rather than as arbitrariness. The error is made easily and avoided with difficulty. One means of achieving clarity is to focus upon a comparison of the first and third umpires and their views of how things work, and to place the comparison in a context of the presumption of innocence as a doctrine close to the heart of due process both as a value or normative tenant and as constitutionality.

The salient feature of the first umpire's view of things was his normative prediction of outcome. He wanted so badly to transcend the limitations of perception and cross into reality *per se* that he took the power for granted. As a consequence of the assumption, he knew how things ought to work. He knew the outcome or, at least, he knew what the outcome would be if everything worked as it should. Some historians, the overwhelming number of advocates of aggressive law enforcement and retributive justice, not to mention other whole populations which share the conventional wisdom, see the world in the same way.

The fundamental view reflected by the third umpire's "They ain't nothin' 'till I calls 'em" is not a focus on outcome. It neither contains nor implies a prediction of any sort about anything. It is less ambitious than a prediction. It is merely a description of procedure. The third ump does not say how things ought to work out. He only says how things work. Behind the plate, for example, he knows it is his job to call every pitch not hit either "ball" or "strike." He knows he will do that and the game will proceed. He does not know or presume to know more than that.

Both as a norm and as an empirical feature of Fifth and Fourteenth Amendment clauses of the *Constitution*, the third umpire's view of things is analogous to substantive due process and to the presumption of innocence as a feature of criminal process in large. The presumption of innocence is not the opposite of the presumption of guilt in that, while the latter is a prediction of outcome, the former is merely a description of procedure. The presumption of innocence does not predict, either explicitly or by implication, that any defendant will be found not guilty. Neither does it predict that any defendant will be found guilty. Akin to the third umpire's approach to calling a game, the presumption of innocence does not focus on outcome. Rather, the focus is on procedure.

As a norm, the presumption of innocence argues that criminal process ought to be structured in ways which reliably test the power of government to prosecute and convict. The power of the state is awesome, especially in comparison to the actual lack of resources on the part of the overwhelming number of criminal defendants. The presumption of innocence is a strategy for redressing that imbalance of resources and power by forcing government to hurdle the obstacles of formal adjudication. Without those obstacles, the state would use its power unimpaired, would run on a flat and clear track, as it were, and convictions would be secured with a frequency approximating inevitability, thereby precluding any substantial degree of reliability.

As an empirical feature of Fifth and Fourteenth Amendment clauses in the *Constitution*, substantive due process has emerged as law (*e.g.*, *Palko*, *Adamson*, *Wolf*, *Griswold*, *Mapp*). The essential argument in these cases has been that legal guarantees are taken to be integral features of the meaning of "due process of law" in the Fourteenth Amendment on a selective basis, namely, the extent to which those guarantees are necessary to the very conception of a free society. "The concept of ordered liberty," as Justice Cardozo wrote in *Palko*, is understood to serve judicially as "a rationalizing principle which gives to discrete instances a proper order and coherence."

Judicial conservatives to the contrary notwithstanding, the concept of ordered liberty as a rationalizing principle governing inclusion or exclusion of specific guarantees within the meaning of due process in the Fourteenth Amendment does not place judges at large any more than the task of umpires calling close plays means that the game of baseball is controlled by umpires acting *ad hoc*. It is the task of an umpire behind the plate, for example, to call balls and strikes, but there is an empirical quality to the strike zone.

Due process, whether as a norm or as an empirical feature of constitutional law, is difficult enough to understand because the entire matter amounts to a convergence of empirical and judgmental entities. When one tries to understand due process, it can be helpful to recognize a common denominator between the concept of ordered liberty as constitutional law and the presumption of innocence as a norm of criminal jurisprudence, *viz.*, neither the concept nor the presumption is a focus upon outcome. Both focus upon procedure.

Through substantive due process in a context of constitutional law, particular guarantees are incorporated or excluded from incorporation under the due process clause of the Fourteenth Amendment. In criminal court proceedings, whether trial courts or appellate courts, particular verdicts of guilt or innocence and particular holdings of affirmation or reversal are forthcoming as case law. If one approaches this array by concentrating upon outcomes, upon verdicts and holdings, due process will appear chaotic or, at least, *ad hoc*. The truth is that the consistency, the rationale, the principle is present but underlying, more real than apparent. The rationale is procedure itself, procedure *per se*, an emphasis upon formal adjudicative obstacles to the raw power of government to prosecute and convict.

That rationale has been found and administered by courts and, in that process, judges have played major roles, but the locus of the rationale has been the *Constitution* and the finding has been far more discovery than invention.

Chapter Five

The Exclusionary Rule: How to Deter the Police From Violating the Constitution

If the constable errs, the criminal goes free.

—*People v. DeFore*,
N.Y. State Court of Appeals (1926)

The material on plea bargaining in earlier chapters of this book approached that topic as a secret hidden in plain sight. The argument went that, when the criminal justice system in the United States is understood as a matter of political economy, plea bargaining becomes the key to unlocking the secrets of the system. Since plea bargaining is the means by which somewhere between three-fourths and nine-tenths of all criminal cases are managed, that would seem to qualify as plain view. Since most if not all conventional analyses of the system either fail to mention plea bargaining or treat it merely as an afterthought or footnote, that would seem to qualify as a secret. When that key is found and used, the system gives up its most fundamental secrets, namely, that it functions primarily to warehouse a portion of the surplus population generated by the political economy, and criminal jurisprudence develops as ideological rationalization for that primary function.

By contrast with plea bargaining as a secret hidden in plain view, the exclusionary rule in criminal law may be characterized as a grain of sand. In most of the early Eastern religions, proverbs asserted that the universe was to be found in a grain of sand. Whether in *Upanishads*, *Tao te Ching*, *Koran*, or *Talmud*, a common image was that providence had revealed itself in the humblest objects. The exclusionary rule is that sort of apparently innocuous piece within which the entire universe of criminal jurisprudence may be revealed.

1. Emergence

In the early years of the nineteenth century, a man named Weeks worked for the railroad in Kansas City, Missouri. The federal marshal in K.C. suspected that Weeks was engaged in illegal gambling activities and using the railroad as a vehicle for furthering his illegal enterprise. At the urging of the marshal and while Weeks was working at the railroad yard, two municipal police officers went to Weeks' rooming house and were given entry to Weeks' room by one of the boarders in the house. Inside Weeks' room, the two police officers noticed what they thought might be evidence of illegal gambling activity and they left everything undisturbed while they returned downtown to inform the marshal of what they had seen. The marshal went to the boarding house in the company of the two K.C. officers, entered Weeks' room as before, searched the room and seized what the marshal considered contraband. Subsequently, Weeks was arrested at the railroad yard, indicted and brought to trial in federal district court. The assistant attorney general prosecuting the case for the U.S. used the evidence seized by the marshal and Weeks was convicted. On appeal, the U.S. Supreme Court granted *certiorari* and, in 1914, handed down their decision in *Weeks v. U.S.* 232 U.S.383.

As is true of every decision by the Court to grant *certiorari* or to review the handling of a case on the part of a lower court by noting probable jurisdiction, the basis for the review was that a minimum of four of the nine members of the court had seen something in the merits or the appellate process to suggest an opportunity for the court to make significant law. In *Weeks*, that opportunity was clear: Had the federal marshal violated the "unreasonable search and seizure" provision of the Fourth Amendment? If not, why not? If he had, what was to be done about it?

The court held that the actions of the federal marshal, in entering a private residence and seizing property without a warrant and in the absence of any emergency, were violations of the Fourth Amendment. Put differently, the court held that if such intrusion was not unreasonable, the Fourth Amendment prohibition prohibited nothing. The other question before the court, which they decided to address as well, was what was to be done about the intrusion to discourage such violations on the part of other federal marshals. The court's answer to that question marked the emergence of the exclusionary rule in American criminal law.

In order to understand the court's response, it is necessary to recall the historicity of the Fourth Amendment. Its framers were convinced that nothing in the original *Constitution of the United States* was sufficiently pointed or emphatic to guarantee an effective prohibition against governmental invasion of the citizen's private property. After all, this had been one of the fundamental issues in the War for Independence, in which the colonists had claimed no more than what they saw as the rights of Englishmen, namely, a right to their own property free from governmental intrusion. In the larger context of the Revolution, the convention of 1787 and ratification of the original constitution in 1789, the same reasoning had charged the historical atmosphere in which the entire Bill of Rights had been proposed and ratified as amendments.

Therefore, the initial question before the court in *Weeks* was no mere footnote. Implicitly, the court asked whether there was any substantial difference in law between quartering British redcoats in the homes of American colonists against the will of the colonists and at the pleasure of the crown, and what the federal marshal had done in Kansas City. Once the court responded to that initial issue by saying, effectively, there was no substantial difference in law under the Fourth Amendment, the court turned to the question of remedy, not in any ordinary atmosphere but as a matter of vital importance to the whole constitutional fabric of the nation.

The court held that the material seized by the marshal in Weeks' room, incident to a warrantless entry absent exigency, ought not to have been considered evidence by the federal district court as trier-of-fact. Since the district court had made a judicial error in admitting the material as evidence, the trial and its verdict were reversed. As regards courts, the implicit admonition from the U.S. Supreme Court in *Weeks* was that a similar fate awaited, namely, reversal. Further, the admonition from the high court was aimed directly and explicitly at deterring unconstitutional activity on the part of federal law enforcement personnel. Those authorities were to obey the Fourth Amendment; if they did not, they would lose the fruit of their labor, namely, evidence they had gathered. Few if any commodities are more prized by law enforcement personnel than evidence of factual guilt of suspects, and all the more so if that evidence has been obtained by the direct activity of the officer.

2. Early Development

The *Weeks* doctrine, as it came to be known, was significant not only for what the court had written but for what the court had not included. The U.S. Supreme Court, reviewing the handling of a case by a federal district court, had seen fit to address the activities of a federal marshal. The court had not seen fit to address any issues regarding the activities of the Kansas City police or the state of Missouri or any of its courts. Clearly, Kansas City police had been involved in the case, therefore, the court might have addressed the issue of local and state police and local and state courts. At their discretion, the court did not do so, and that discretionary call became the context in which the early development of the exclusionary rule took place.

By their not having addressed the potential issue of *Weeks* sanctions with regard to the states, the court had begged two questions: (1) Was the Fourth Amendment attached to the states? Did the provisions of the Fourth Amendment restrain local and state police and such courts? (2) Was the exclusionary rule merely a judicial innovation of remedy adopted by the *Weeks* court or was the rule penumbral, thus, fundamental, in the context of the Fourth Amendment so that the rule attached wherever the Amendment attached? The first of those questions was more obvious but the second was no less significant and, over time, might prove even more intimately involved with constitutional criminal procedure.

Shortly after *Weeks* was handed down, the "silver platter" doctrine emerged. Basically, this doctrine held that all that was necessary in order to be able to use material seized in violation of the Fourth Amendment in federal court was to see to it that the search and seizure had been carried out by some local or state officer. The doctrine remained in effect in the United States from *Weeks* from 1914 to 1960. For almost half a century, in other words, information, which was barred from being used in federal courts because of the manner in which it was seized by federal officers, was admissable in federal courts on a silver platter of state seizure and, of course, admissable in local and state courts at the discretion of those courts. Considering the development of the United States from the first year of the outbreak of World War I in Europe to the year in which John Fitzgerald Kennedy was elected president, the longevity of the silver platter begs analysis.

One explanation of the durability of the silver platter doctrine was that it hinged upon resolution of the other issue raised in *Weeks*, namely, the question of whether the Fourth Amendment was attached in restraint of the states. This explanation would imply that resolution of the Fourth Amendment incorporation issue was a prerequisite to resolving issues raised by the silver platter. That is a decent argument in law and, as it turned out, an accurate prediction. The silver platter was put aside after the Fourth Amendment had been held fundamental to the concept of ordered liberty, thus, to be incorporated under the terms of the Fourteenth Amendment due process clause in restraint of the states. The difficulty of using that explanation as the entire account, however, is that the silver platter was not abandoned until eleven years following resolution of the incorporation issue. If the silver platter was no more than a hinge on the door of Fourth Amendment incorporation, why did the hinge not swing as the door opened? What took so long?

The answer to that question raises another of the truly fundamental components of constitutional law in the United States, namely, federalism. The proposed constitution drafted in Philadelphia during the summer of 1787 had been ratified into the supreme law of the land by the states. Therein lies the origin of federalism and one of the most profound though frequently overlooked truths about criminal procedure. In ratifying the proposed constitution, the states had surrendered enormous powers to the central government established by ratification. History does not offer many examples of political and governmental entities voluntarily surrendering their powers, but that is exactly what occured in North America between the convention in 1787 and 1789 when the new government under Washington took office. What made it possible?

The proposal from the convention amounted to a bargain or implicit contract, the terms of which were greatly enhanced stability, particularly in the conduct of commerce, in exchange for the surrender of state prerogatives. Though there were many in the several states who argued against ratification, the states went for the bargain. They valued enhanced stability more highly than the powers they abandoned. However, the states placed a contingency on their acceptance.

The contingency was that the states reserved the right to draft and ratify amendments to the proposed constitution. It was to be understood, with the understanding taking the form of a gentlemen's agreement, that such amendments as might be proposed were to become an important part of the early work of the central government under the Constitution. Ten amendments were drafted and ratified between 1789 and 1791. We know them as the Bill of Rights. They were ten reasonably specific prohibitions against the power of the newly established central government, limitations which garnered sufficient enthusiasm in the states to be ratified as parts of the supreme law of the land. Consider the grain of sand metaphor here.

Constitutional criminal jurisprudence in the United States has developed since 1789 largely in a context of the Bill of Rights and the Fourteenth Amendment. The Bill of Rights dug a channel for that development, marking its direction not toward enhanced governmental powers but toward limiting the powers of government to secure criminal convictions. Furthermore, the Bill of Rights guaranteed that government in the United States would consist of those powers reserved locally and to the states, those reserved exclusively as powers of the central government, and those powers shared by state and federal authorities. That arrangement of the three forms of powers is called federalism. It is as central to the Constitution as any other aspect, therefore, it remains essential to constitutional criminal jurisprudence in the United States. That was an important consideration on the part of the court when they considered whether to extend to the states the exclusionary sanction adopted in *Weeks* to restrain federal officers. To put it differently, that is what took so long.

In a Colorado case which the U.S. Supreme Court handed down in 1949, *Wolf v. Colorado* 338 U.S.25, the court incorporated the Fourth Amendment as attached to the states by the provisions of the Fourteenth Amendment due process clause. The court had established the jurisprudential base from which *Wolf* was reasoned in two earlier cases. In *Weeks*, the court had emphasized the importance of Fourth Amendment guarantees by applying the exclusionary rule as a remedy for violations. In *Palko v. Connecticut*, 302 U.S.319 (1937), the Court laid the foundation for incorporating any guarantee found in the U.S. Constitution, whether found explicitly or by implication as ". . . immunities that are valid as against the federal government by force of the specific pledges of amendments have been found to be implicit in the concept of ordered liberty, and thus, through the Fourteenth Amendment, become valid as against the states." [*Palko*, *supra*.]

Interestingly, the Court in Palko had refused to incorporate either the specific prohibition against double jeopardy in the Fifth Amendment or the entirety of the Bill of Rights as constitutional provisions attached to the states. This was a Connecticut case in which that state had permitted the prosecution to retry Palko on a capital charge on the grounds that the jury in the initial trial had returned only a verdict of murder, second degree, which had precluded the death penalty, and that the jury had been mislead by improper instructions as well as other judicial errors on the part of the trial court. Writing for the Court in *Palko*, Justice Cardozo explicated "the concept of ordered liberty" as "a rationalizing principle which gives to discrete instances a proper order and coherence." Palko's appeal was heard but his argument denied, while the Court established ordered liberty as the jurisprudential rubric according to which specific guarantees in the Bill of Rights, explicitly as in the double jeopardy prohibition or implicitly as, for example, privacy claims, were to be found and attached in restraint against the states.

In its decision in *Wolf*, the Court for the first time attached the restraint of the Fourth Amendment to the states.

> The security of one's privacy against arbitrary intrusion by the police—which is at the core of the Fourth Amendment—is basic to a free society. It is therefore implicit in "the concept of ordered liberty" and as such enforceable against the States through the Due Process clause.

However, the *Wolf* Court explicitly refused to extend the exclusionary rule along with the Amendment.

> We hold, therefore, that in a prosecution in a State court for a State crime the Fourteenth Amendment does not forbid the admission of evidence obtained by an unreasonable search and seizure.

Four years after the court handed down *Wolf*, Earl Warren became Chief Justice of the United States Supreme Court and, under his aegis, a jurisprudential revolution of sorts was to occur. No single factor nor set of factors accounts entirely for any revolution and, for that matter, it can be argued that revolution is always an uninformed metaphor for developments which were in fact evolutionary. But what took place in constitutional law in the United States from 1953 to 1971, the years while Warren was chief justice, was nothing short of monumental. No chief justice but John Marshall compares with Warren for the magnitude of work product. No court in history compares favorably with the Warren court for the frequency and impact of its decisions: one-man-one-vote reapportionment, an end to separate-but-equal in favor of separate-is-inherently-unequal and, in criminal jurisprudence, the rights of indigents to post-conviction appeal and to counsel during trial and during custodial interrogation. By the sixties, at least one candidate for the presidency ran on a domestic platform which included reversing decisions of the Warren court by congressional action, and calls for the impeachment of the chief justice had appeared in every state. If the years 1953 through 1971 for the Court were not revolutionary, they were neither innocuous nor ordinary.

The overwhelming significance of the Court during the years when Earl Warren was chief justice recommend some sort of account. Much has been written and more has been argued which has been claptrap and hyperbole, and an essay on the exclusionary rule seems an unlikely context to attempt any comprehensive explanation of the Warren Court. Still, in that Court's most important decisions there was an underlying jurisprudential thread which has been ignored or undervalued by those few who have commented on it at all. Then, too, it would be a blatant omission in this book because that underlying jurisprudential line is connected intimately with the political economic argument here.

Of course, the mere mechanism of the court, whereby law can be made by a vote of five against four, was crucial to the output of the Warren court. The chief knew he enjoyed a reliable majority: Hugo Black, William J. Brennan, Thurgood Marshall and then, depending upon retirements and appointments and who was sitting during a particular session, William O. Douglas, Tom Clark, and the Goldberg-Fortas seat. Earl Warren was too polite to crow publicly but he was more than enough politician to appreciate the votes he had in his pocket. But that mere mechanism does not account for the work product. It does not explain the direction of the Warren court, particularly, though not entirely, in criminal jurisprudence. What does offer a promising avenue along which the answers may be pursued is to recognize that the Warren Court majority over those eighteen years had discovered a profound truth about the law. It was another of the truths hidden in plain view.

Whether reapportionment or school desegregation, whether the right of convicted felons to appeal or the right of suspect and defendants to counsel and to the privilege against compulsory self-incrimination, the jurisprudence of the Warren Court emerged from its discovery of poverty in the United States as a material fact and an issue central to justice. When, during the third session of Warren's tenure, the Court wrote that ". . . the kind of justice a man gets ought not to depend upon the amount of money he has . . ." the Court announced that an indigent convicted and incarcerated had the same right to appeal as that available to felons who were not indigent [*Griffin v. Illinois*, 351 U.S.12 (1956). The Court was using the fundamental jurisprudential argument of due process fairness which it used in nearly every one of its major decisions: *Suum quoque tribuere*, to-one-as-to-all.

As jurisprudence, to-one-as-to-all argued that the historical and material circumstance of poverty, referred to in law as indigency and defined as an inability to hire an attorney, had become a central issue in American criminal justice. Unless the Court was to underwrite, as courts before had done, a two-tiered system of justice, one for the wealthy and quite another for the poor, the Court was obliged to intervene in the collision of citizenry and government on the side of those who had been condemned historically by their poverty to tawdry and dismal justice. The Court applied that same jurisprudence in 1963 when it established an indigent's right to appointed counsel during felony trial [*Gideon v. Wainwright*, 372 U.S.335], and again in the controversial cases of *Escobedo v. Illinois,* 378 U.S.478 (1964) and *Miranda v. Arizona,* 384 U.S.436 (1966), each decided by a five-to-four vote, in which the court established an indigent's right to counsel (*Escobedo*) and to silence (*Miranda*) during custodial interrogation. *Suum quoque tribuere* was not peculiar to the Warren Court, but no Court before or since used it as consistently and as emphatically in as many decisions which had such major impacts.

To be sure, as Warren Court critics have insisted and as subsequent courts under Warren Burger and William Rehnquist have ruled, to-one-as-to-all applied to the rich as well as to the poor. Anatole France had said much the same in observing that the law, in its impartiality, forbids the rich as well as the poor from sleeping under bridges.

What the Warren Court majority recognized, with regard to segregated public facilities, apportionment, and criminal process, was that such guarantees as effective assistance of counsel are meaningful only for the poor. No wealthy person would consider going anywhere near a criminal court on a charge without benefit of the finest legal counsel money could obtain. The state would not consider going into court to prosecute without assistance of the best trained legal staff it required. It was the poor for whom any of this had been at issue, and the Warren Court attempted to mitigate the imbalance.

In 1960, the Warren Court ended the silver platter doctrine in *Elkins v. U.S.* 364 U.S.206, then the following year extended the exclusionary rule in restraint against the states. The case was *Mapp v. Ohio*, 367 U.S.643 (1961).

> Since the Fourth Amendment's right of privacy has been declared enforceable against the States through the Due Process clause of the Fourteenth, it is enforceable against them by the same sanction of exclusion as is used against the Federal Government.

To appreciate *Mapp* in the context of the exclusionary rule and its early development, it is necessary to recall that the criminal justice system in the United States is funded, arranged, organized and staffed largely at the local and state level rather than at the federal level. When the Court in *Mapp* extended the exclusionary rule to the states, the court for the first made the rule applicable to ninety-five percent of the criminal justice system.

3. Later Development

If the underlying theme of to-one-as-to-all marked development of criminal jurisprudence during the era of the Warren Court, another current, often related to *suum quoque tribuere*, carried the Warren Court's handling of the exclusionary rule. The Court was concerned about the extent and degree of unevenness in the American system of criminal justice. While the Court did not command authority or resources necessary for a frontal assault on unevenness, the Court never lost sight of the phenomenon as a basic issue.

Put starkly, the issue of unevenness was the fact that what happened in matters of criminal justice in one jurisdiction was not what happened in another. Of course, the fundamental basis for that unevenness was federalism. The Warren Court's handling of *Mapp* was the most significant case in point. In extending the exclusionary rule to the ninety-five percent of the American criminal justice system previously not covered by it, the Warren Court was attempting, by judicial remedy, to bring state courts up to snuff. By and large, when the Warren Court saw an opportunity to admonish state courts to meet the same norms of jurisprudence as those obliged throughout the federal judiciary, the Court took it and it had done just that in *Mapp*.

Seven years later, and with the *Escobedo* and *Miranda* decisions having incurred the wrath of the law enforcement community during those seven years, the Warren court handed down a decision in an Ohio case which police officers found to their liking. In the case, a Cleveland police officer with more than thirty years experience had observed three men on a public street who were behaving in a manner the cop saw as reasonable suspicion that they were about to rob a store. The officer intervened before any such event occured and, in order to protect himself, he patted down the outer clothing of the three, whereupon he found two concealed weapons. Once he had secured the weapons, the officer had probable cause and with it he carried out a more extensive search of the three and placed them under arrest. Their convictions were appealed on the grounds of an illegal search and seizure because, at the time of the initial pat down, they had done nothing criminal. The Warren Court saw in those merits an opportunity to rule on an a circumstance crucial to criminal justice, namely, the initial confrontation between police and citizenry on the streets.

In *Terry v. Ohio*, 392 U.S. 1, (1968), the Court held that a cursory pat down—a stop 'n' frisk in the vernacular—for the purpose of protecting an officer's safety and upon reasonable, articulable suspicion that a criminal offense was or was about to be committed, did not violate the Fourth Amendment and that, therefore, use of weapons seized during such a cursory pat down did not violate the exclusionary rule applicable to the states as a result of *Mapp*. As the Court saw it, any other ruling would put a police officer at unacceptable risk every time there was a reasonable basis to intervene in the behavior of citizens on the street.

Terry has been misunderstood since it was announced. The essential thing to notice in *Terry* is that it was a narrow exception to the exclusionary rule. Once that narrowness is appreciated as an exception to the rule, the decision becomes clear. Also since *Terry*, attorneys and courts have been pursuing the generic dimension of exceptions *per se*, and that has been the underlying theme of the later and more recent development of the rule.

In a 1983 decision, *U.S. v. Leon*, 468 U.S.897, the Court then under the aegis of Warren Burger, ruled that police officers who had acquired reasonable suspicion of illegal drug activity through observations of citizens, and who had sworn in affidavit to those observations with a prosecutor, and who had gone with the prosecutor to a magistrate to secure a search warrant, and had been given a warrant by that magistrate on the basis of their affidavit, were entitled to search under the terms of the warrant even though an appellate court had held subsequently that the warrant ought not to have been granted and that it had been illegal *prima facie*—on its face. The Court held that questions concerning the affidavit and warrant required legal expertise not reasonably within the scope of police responsibilities, and that the exclusionary rule had been established and developed only as a means of deterring unconstitutional activity by police, not deterring judicial error. The police had operated in good faith as they had conducted their investigation and followed the process of obtaining a warrant. Any legal errors committed by magistrates as officers of the court during that process did not invalidate the good faith of the police.

The so-called *Leon* good-faith rule, announcing another exception to the exclusionary rule, became a favorite of police. As Warren Burger gave way as chief justice to the man who had been one of his mainstays as an associate justice, William J. Rehnquist, the Court became more emphatic about the quest for exceptions to the exclusionary rule. As the personnel on the Court became more conservative, opposition to the exclusionary rule mounted. Moreover, the chief justice was more concerned over inefficient administration of the federal judiciary than the Warren Court had been over unevenness. Chief Justice Rehnquist has proven to be one of the most able administrators of the courts in its entire history. The historical jury is still out with regard to what Rehnquist's attention to administrative issues may have cost in terms of justice, but there is no denying the enhanced efficiency.

Rehnquist's quest for a more efficient judiciary has taken two main forms. In one, he has reduced and continues to attempt to reduce the workload of the federal courts. If fewer appeals are carried to the federal courts from the states, and if fewer appeals within federal law are permitted, the caseload declines. That is precisely what has occured and by the primary tactic of limiting the use of *habeas corpus*. The Latin literally means to present the body, and it became a staple in the development of Anglo-American criminal law as a means of precluding star chamber proceedings. In more practical terms, *habeas* has come to be understood as protestation over the conditions of confinement. Consequently, most *habeas* petitions emerge from local and state jails and prisons and from federal prisons. What Rehnquist has done with the federal courts has been to restrict the number of *habeas* petitions a federal inmate is allowed, and to encourage state courts to adopt a similar approach.

In his other administrative policy, a matter which neither the chief justice nor the court as such will acknowledge, Rehnquist and his majority have drugs and drug-related cases as exceptions to the exclusionary rule. To appreciate the court's unofficial policy as a matter of enhancing administrative efficiency, consider that drug and drug-related cases now constitute something on the order of half of all criminal cases at the local, state and federal levels. Anything which chips away effectively on the volume of drug cases or on their disposition will be important as a means of reducing overall caseload in the courts. By discouraging use of the exclusionary rule, courts do not decrease caseload immediately. However, by securing conviction in federal courts on charges of violations of federal drug laws, some of the people manufacturing, distributing and using drugs will be incarcerated, thus, incapacitated from contributing further to the caseload. Then, too, the policy is likely to be approved by conservatives in the judiciary, Congress and state legislatures, and the fundamentalist-oriented portion of the public because of the manner in which draconian incarceration fits into advocacy of retributive justice. Hammurabi's Code did not cease with the decline of Mesopotamia.

The unofficial policy in the federal courts has received considerable approval elsewhere on the part of courts, other agencies of government, and the portion of the public who have become aware of the policy. Unofficial, unacknowledged and denied, the policy remains that adopting the exclusionary rule in drug cases will be more difficult, especially in federal courts, than using the rule in cases which do not involve drugs. A recent decision by the Rehnquist Court will illustrate one of the ways in which the judicial war on drugs is being conducted.

The case was *Hodari D.* 111 S.Ct. 1547 (1991). Two Oakland, California police officers were patrolling a high-crime neighborhood in their cruiser. As they turned a corner they spotted a car at the curb, lights on and engine running, with five or six teenagers crouched beside the driver's side. When the teenagers noticed the police car, the car sped away and the teenagers ran in different directions. The officers decided to chase one particular teen and one officer drove the car slowly pursuing from the rear while the other officer ran on foot around the corner and through an alley attempting to head off the kid. While running, the teenager seemed occupied with the police car behind him to the extent that he did not notice the officer approaching on foot from his front until only a matter of yards separated the two. When the teenager realized an officer was coming straight toward him on foot, the kid threw an object into the street. A second or two later, the officer on foot tackled the teenager. The officers recovered the discarded object which turned out to be crack-cocaine and the teenager, Hodari D., was taken into custody, the California Juvenile Justice version of an arrest.

The cocaine was admitted by the trial court and Hodari was convicted. On appeal, defense counsel argued that the seizure of Hodari's property had been unconstitutional because the police lacked probable cause and a warrant. The United States Supreme Court granted review and offered a somewhat novel argument in affirming Hodari's conviction and the trial court's admission of the cocaine. The Court held there had been no seizure in Fourth Amendment terms because, at the moment Hodari had discarded the cocaine, he had not been taken into custody, therefore, the police were entitled to retrieve what was no more than abandoned property.

Hodari D. represents an indirect but effective reduction in the scope of the exclusionary rule. The Court precluded the rule by precluding the Fourth Amendment issue within the merits of the case.

4. Analysis

The development of the exclusionary rule in the United States reflects two fundamental issues: (1) Is the rule truly fundamental as a penumbra of the Fourth Amendment, or is the rule merely a judicial innovation? (2) In view of the controversy surrounding the rule, what options seem to recommend themselves?

Are there alternatives to the exclusionary rule?

Since the *Weeks* Court first announced the exclusionary rule, controversy has surrounded its application. Use of the exclusionary rule has been subjected to searing and extensive cost/benefit analysis over the years: What seem to be the benefits accruing from use of the rule with regard to the stated aim of deterring unconsitutional activity on the part of the police, and how do those results compare with the costs to judges and juries as triers-of-fact? Cost/benefit arguments over the rule have not persuaded very many people other then those who needed no persuasion because they had decided beforehand. Still, cost/benefit analysis does reveal one of the fundamental issues about the rule, namely, when a court of original jurisdiction in a criminal case, state or federal court, operates as a trier-of-fact, use of the exclusionary rule—granting a motion to suppress certain data—can be conclusive. Use of the rule can come close to determining the outcome of an entire case. Consider one dramatic illustration.

In 1968 in Iowa a man named Robert Williams was tried for the murder of a ten-year old girl he had kidnapped and buried in a shallow grave. The circumstances were, stark: Williams was black and an escaped mental patient. The little girl was white and had been abducted on Christmas Eve from a Y.M.C.A. event in Des Moines. On advice of counsel, Williams surrendered himself to police in Davenport, Iowa, where he was given his *Miranda* admonitions not less than three times. As officers arrived in Davenport from Des Moines to take Williams back to their jurisdiction under terms of an arrest warrant, and again on advice of counsel, Williams was warned not to speak to the officers during the ride and the officers were admonished not to interrogate Williams during the ride in the absence of counsel who had asked and been refused permission to go along in the cruiser. Shortly after leaving Davenport, Captain Cleatus Leaming, Des Moines P.D., delivered what the court was to refer to subsequently as "the Christian burial" speech. The gist of Leaming's remarks was to encourage Williams to take the officers to where he had hidden the little girl's body in order that her family could give her a decent Christian burial. Williams did just that, and he was convicted in an Iowa trial court and the conviction was affirmed by the Iowa Supreme Court.

A federal district court and the Fourth Circuit U.S. Court of Appeals reversed the conviction on grounds that Williams' confession had been obtained by post-arrest custodial interrogation in the absence of counsel. The U.S.Supreme Court granted *certiorari* and determined that the issue in the case was whether there was any clear indication in the record of a valid waiver by Williams of his right to counsel. Finding no such indication, the court, five to four, affirmed the federal courts and vacated Williams' conviction. The court argued that the confession and its fruits, including the corpse of the little girl, ought never to have been admitted as evidence in the trial court. The case was *Brewer v. Williams*, 430 U.S.387 (1977).

It would be difficult if not impossible to find, in all the annals of American criminal jurisprudence, any single case which more clearly reveals the costs which can accompany use of the exclusionary rule. Chief Justice Burger dissented vigorously, along with three associate justices. Burger's dissent reached what was for him unusual eloquence: "What the court has done today fulfills Justice Cardozo's grim prophecy that, one day, a court would discard the body of a murder victim because of the manner in which it had been found." That was precisely what the *Brewer* Court had done,

It must be noted that, while vacating his original conviction, the court in *Brewer* attached a memorandum to the Iowa courts, informing state authorities of how they could bring Williams to trial and secure a conviction without using any of the evidence excluded. The Iowa courts followed that advice to the letter and, in *Nix v. Williams*, 467 U.S.431 (1984), Chief Justice Burger writing for the majority, the Court affirmed Williams' *de novo* conviction on charges of having murdered the little girl. Williams is serving a sentence of life without possibility of parole.

But *Nix* does not detract from the effectiveness of *Brewer* as an illustration of the costs which can accompany use of the exclusionary rule. The illustration highlights the question of options.

To reiterate, the exclusionary rule has been aimed at deterring unconstitutional activity on the part of the police. Are there no more effective means of deterrence than to vacate criminal convictions? Many alternatives to the rule have been recommended over the years since *Weeks*. These include direct punishment of offending officers in such forms as loss of salary, loss of retirement benefits, reductions in rank, and the like. While advocates of these options tend to regard their proposals as panaceas, three salient facts remain: Courts seldom enjoy jurisdiction over the particular matters these proposed alternatives to the exclusionary rule imply. The U.S. Supreme Court, for example, does not command the salary, promotional, and retirement package of the San Francisco Police Department, and the court would have a difficult time, if it proved possible at all, in using such matters as effective sanctions. Secondly, the issue of proposed alternatives to the exclusionary rule almost always fails to take into account the simple fact that no such alternative has ever been implemented. The exclusionary rule has been the only judicially imposed sanction to deter unconstitutional activity on the part of the police since the rule was announced in 1914.

Then, too, there is a distinction lost on the larger number of law students as well as the public at large. It is a distinction between unconstitutional activity and criminal activity. To see it, consider the following illustration. Nowhere in the United States, not in a single one of the more than 20,000 police jurisdictions throughout the United States, will there be found a criminal charge, misdemeanor or felony, which prohibits and penalizes police officers for failure to administer proper *Miranda* admonitions. Improper *Miranda* warnings are a constitutional rather than a criminal matter. The exclusionary rule deters such unconstitutional activity by threatening to eliminate the fruit of a criminal investigation from the prosecution's evidence in court.

It would be wise for those who argue in favor of alternatives to the rule to consider the distinction and connection between history and logic. Alternatives are proposed always from logical grounds whereas the rule and its development have been primarily historical. As Steinbeck wrote in his *Log from the Sea of Cortez*, with history, "either all of it matters or none of it, and it all matters." History is always real, always important, always consequential. It seldom is logical. The logic surrounding the formation and development of the exclusionary rule is every bit as shaky as the logic which has underwritten federalism in the United States. In both instances, history has been far more the logic of experience rather than the experience of logic, to use a phrase favored by both Holmes and John Dewey.

Is the exclusionary rule fundamental?

Penumbras in constitutional law are understood to be implications reasonably drawn from explicit guarantees. The word "privacy" does not appear in the U.S. Constitution but few Americans would argue that the right has not been guaranteed there. Moreover, an entire jurisprudence of privacy has developed in American criminal jurisprudence since *Boyd v. U.S.*, 116 U.S.616 (1886). Privacy is a penumbral right in constitutional criminal law. Indeed, in the context of the Fourth Amendment, the penumbra of privacy has been central. Along with the Fifth Amendment provision prohibiting compulsory self-incrimination, the Fourth Amendment has been the constitutional locus of privacy jurisprudence as it was the locus of the original announcement of the exclusionary rule. Some justices, judges and legal scholars have argued that the rule is every bit as fundamental or penumbral as privacy or any other implication drawn from the explicit portions of the Bill of Rights. Most have not, and that is the question here.

As a third consideration on this issue of alternatives to the exclusionary rule, it is important to realize, as so few people including law students do realize, that there is a difference between unconstitutional and criminal activities. For instance, there is not a single one among the more than 20,000 police jurisdictions throughout the United States in which it is a crime, misdemeanor or felony, to violate the U.S. Constitution, *e.g.*, failure of a police officer to administer proper *Miranda* admonitions. Subsequently, courts may hold that such behavior on the part of the officer was unconstitutional and, on that account, suppress material gathered, but the officer cannot be indicted on a criminal charge on that account. Getting such potential criminal charges on the books would be a local process, extremely unlikely anywhere and virtually impossible everywhere in a uniform fashion.

Whether the exclusionary rule is penumbral or merely a judicial innovation is a question which requires understanding the historical development of American constitutional criminal jurisprudence. The answer requires as well a practical appreciation of the demands and restrictions placed upon law enforcement in the United States. Thus, it is not a question to be answered easily or quickly. It is the sort of question which recalls the grain of sand metaphor. In attempting to answer it, one must involve oneself in analysis of far more than the exclusionary rule. It is one of those questions which is productive less because of any particular answer or side taken than because of the developing argument. Consider the following distinction.

What is the essential difference between discovery and invention? Geographically, for instance, did explorers discover or invent the North American continent? They may be said to have bumped into it but was it discovery or invention? Discovery, of course, for it had been there all along waiting, if you will, to be found.

Did the *Weeks* Court discover or invent the exclusionary rule? Since the rule was announced in 1914 for the first time as a feature of American constitutional criminal procedure, had the rule been waiting in the Constitution and its Amendments? The Fourth Amendment prohibits unreasonable search and seizure. Regardless of how the meaning of "unreasonable" has developed, does the prohibition *per se* carry an implication of a remedy to be attached to violating the prohibition? Parents, teachers, indeed, people responsible for the behavior of other people everywhere, learn on the job quickly that it is unwise to prohibit something and then not back up the prohibition with a penalty attached to violation. Does that apply to constitutional law?

If the exclusionary rule was merely an *ad hoc* innovation on the part of the *Weeks* Court, then it is not penumbral. Rather, the rule exists to be applied or not according to the discretion of the courts using a cost/benefit formula. When the costs of applying suppression outweigh the deterrence, the exclusionary rule is not to be imposed. Where the reverse seems the case, the rule is to be imposed. Many are quick to respond, "that is exactly what happens," but what happens may not be right, eh? After all, the entire Enlightenment of the eighteenth century was arrayed against, "whatever is, is right," wrote Alexander Pope.

5. Postscript

Law, always and everywhere, is a matter of social control, whatever else it may be anywhere. Whether law is generated legislatively or judicially, whether it comes in the form of statutes or jurisprudence, the process of law involves necessarily the deeper matter of social development. There are no guarantees, in law or elsewhere, that social development will be wise, humane, sensitive to needs or just, but the very nature of law as social process does insure that the law will reflect whatever development has marked the society in which it is made. Consider the following illustrations in the context of the exclusionary rule:

During February, 1995, the U.S. Supreme Court, in the case of *Arizona v. Evans*, (No.93-1660), in a seven-to-two holding, announced that police were entitled to proceed on the terms of a warrant even though they had relied on a court-generated computer report which had been programmed in error. The key was an extension of the *Leon* good-faith exception. As long as the error had been made by officers of the court and not by the police, and the police had proceeded in good faith, errors on the computer report did not invalidate search and seizure. *Evans* was another drug case.

At this writing, with the enthusiastic support of the newly-elected Speaker, the House of Representatives overwhelmingly passed a bill which, should it ever become law, would extend the *Leon* exception far beyond anything the court did in *Evans*. The House bill holds that, as long as the police act in good faith and believe they do not require a warrant for search and/or arrest, no warrant may be required, thus, no issue of suppression may be raised. I can state categorically that, in more than a quarter century of professional work associated with the law, I have yet to encounter a single officer who did not believe himself to have acted in good faith.

Chapter Six

Reflections on the Rodney King Case

From the time a guy puts on the uniform and steps out of the academy, an erosion process begins to take place. Some guys are able to deal with it and cope with it fine. They pop out the other end no worse for wear. That's very, very rare. The vast majority of policemen are eroded by their environment, by the people and the places they work in. They become reflections of the people they police . . . (246)[1]

1. A Challenge to Convention

The young woman came into my office as she had many times previously. She had completed two courses with me and currently was enrolled in a third. During those courses, we had come to recognize several important social and legal issues about which we disagreed, and we had spent time discussing other considerations on which we were of one mind. More importantly than the particulars, we had come to respect one another.

She sat down across from my desk and, simultaneously, as I took one look at her face and reached for the box of tissues I keep in my desk drawer, she asked me for something to wipe her tears.

After a moment or two of silence during which she wiped her eyes and seemed to gather herself for a conversation, she said I was one of the few people she was willing to allow to see her cry. Then she said that she had been on the street protesting all night and had come away from the experience with a throat sore from screaming and a profound sense of frustration.

"There's no one to yell at, nothing to do which will have any effect. The verdict of the jury was so outrageous and there doesn't seem anything can be done."

She was speaking of the Simi Valley jury which had returned acquittals in all but one count on which they had hung in the case against four Los Angeles police officers accused in the beating of Rodney King. While the conversation which ensued will remain the private property of the two people who were involved, the subject of this writing is the events which had occasioned that conversation as well as sub-

1 From, Mark Baker, *Cops: Their Lives in Their Own Words*, (Simon and Schuster, 1985).

sequent happenings directly related, all of which have transformed the entire matter into something at once personal and public, immediate and long-term, concrete and abstract.

It is not a subject about which I write merely to write, or, in any fashion because of a sense of obligation to write about a current subject of significance which falls within my academic and professional expertise. Indeed, the latter consideration made me hesitant lest I do no more than repeat what other so-called experts had said and written. I write in this matter because I have a point of view to offer which I have not heard expressed entirely by anyone else.

To come at it straightaway, I challenge the assumption that the crux of the Rodney King case is racism. In my view the case revolves around two issues linked inextricably by the circumstances: One of those issues is the nature of policing in the United States, and that topic includes the history of policing, its scope and demands, and most particularly, the recruitment and training of police in our society. The second issue which the Rodney King case has begged is legal in its nature. In the actual circumstances of the case, the legal issue is intertwined with the issue of policing but, when that issue is taken in its fullest significance, it may be appreciated beyond and independently of the King case, and the same holds true for the issue of policing. Circumstantially, that is, in the sense that it pertains to the facts of the present case, the legal issue has two specific aspects: the change of venue from Superior Court, City and County of Los Angeles to Superior Court, (Simi Valley) Ventura County, and the privilege against self-incrimination in the Fifth Amendment applicable only metaphorically in the King case and reflected in the decision on the part of the prosecution not to have the victim take the stand.

In challenging the assumption that the Rodney King case centers on racism, I do not challenge the existence or importance of racism as a pervasive fact of life in the United States, indeed, throughout the world. Black Americans or, as the term may be preferred, African Americans, are obliged by nothing less powerful than history to live in the wake of slavery and in the midst of a society which has never healed the racial wounds which helped tear it asunder in 1861. Just as mere words cannot express adequately the horrendous reality that was the American Civil War, neither can anyone put into words the numbing, day-to-day lifetime reality of racism in the United States. Such topics are goals toward which eloquence must strive rather than subjects which the most eloquent scholars can and have conveyed in all the reality.

However, while racism is an integral and pervasive feature of life in the United States, arresting the development of those who advocate and expound it differently to be sure but no less profoundly than those who oppose it or are its targets, racism is neither the only fact of life nor a subject which explains every other fact of life. Single-minded ideology which focuses rhetorically upon any one theme as panacea or as the only matter deserving attention subverts more than it enhances intellectual or social development. To put it simply, racism is a fact of life which can be pointed at accurately to explain, wholly or in part, an array of significant issues in our society, but racism, for all its importance, is not a fact which explains every other fact and issue. Here, I am arguing that racism does not explain either what the Los Angeles police officers did to Rodney King or the verdict of the Simi Valley jury in that case. In searching for an explanation of those events, I have found two considerations, distinguishable from one another in other contexts but, in the King case, bound together by circumstances. Those considerations are, one, police recruitment and training in the United States and, two, specific legal issues of change of venue and a decision on the part of the prosecution not to have the victim in a case take the stand to testify.

2. Venue and the Privilege

Since the happenstance videotape of the Rodney King beating appeared first in the media, attention has been given without effective or noteworthy objection to Rodney King's ethnicity, to his race, rather than to the police officers who were shown in that tape to have beaten King severely. Indeed, far more attention has been paid to King's race than to the circumstances which culminated in those police officers chasing and stopping him in his car that evening in Los Angeles.

I was in my car at the moment that KCBS radio, San Francisco, broadcast the actual reading of the verdict in the King case. The repetitious reading by the clerk required no less than five-plus minutes of air-time. As I drove toward my home across the Golden Gate bridge and listened to those judgments, I was stunned, amazed, perplexed. Had the broadcast been any version other than the actual in-court reading by the court clerk, I would have thought a radio version of a typographical error had been committed. As I listened, I found the verdicts literally incredible on the evidence. The videotape was the evidence. Along with everyone I knew and millions of people whom I did not know, I had seen the evidence in that criminal case, and I had no reasonable explanation for the discrepancy between the evidence and the verdict.

During the two days since the verdict came in, I have paid attention to every scrap of information available in the media on the twelve members of the King jury. I have been occupied during those forty-eight hours with my reflections on the entire matter. I now have an explanation which strikes me as reasonable:

When the California Court of Appeals granted a change of venue, those judges had decided that the nature of the charges against the four police officers, and the media publicity given the videotape of the incident which had occasioned those charges, had precluded the *voir dire* process of jury selection in Los Angeles County from arriving at twelve impartial citizens who could attend a fair presentation of the evidence and respond with integrity as the triers-of-fact. In its attempt to be fair to the case for the People, City and County of Los Angeles as well as to the defense, granting the change of venue was laudatory.

But when the California Court of Appeals changed the venue from Los Angeles County Superior Court to a Ventura County Superior Court, specifically, to a Superior Court in Simi Valley, the Court of Appeals failed in its jurisprudential obligation to insure a jury representative of the population in the original jurisdiction. It would have been possible, for example, to have changed the venue from Los Angeles to San Jose, perhaps to Fresno or even to San Francisco, where *voir dire* would have been administered among a mixed and urban population. A jury in a Simi Valley court was guaranteed to be far more homogenous.

In fact, the jury in the King case came from homes in Simi Valley, a community 40 miles from Los Angeles, and from Oxnard and Ventura, another 30 miles from downtown L.A. Half the jury were women and the youngest of the twelve was 38 while the most senior was 65.

The prosecutor who addressed the court and jury determined, based on his best professional judgment, that putting Rodney King on the stand was an unacceptable risk. Speculations have been plentiful. However, as I watched Rodney King during his first public statement since the trial ended, I had no doubt whatever as to the generic reasons for the prosecutor's decision and, had I been the assistant district attorney prosecuting that case, I would have arrived at the same decision: Putting King on the stand to testify against the police officers who beat him would have made him vulnerable to cross-examination by defense counsel for those officers. Rodney King struck me as nervous, inarticulate, and unable to protect himself even with effective assistance of counsel from the liabilities inherent in the rules of formal adjudication.

Since the verdict was read in the Simi Valley court, a number of armchair quarterbacks have second-guessed the prosecutor's decision not to put King on the stand. Their argument, by and large, has been that the verdict could not have been any worse for the prosecution. Of course, the prosecutor did not have the advantage of hindsight.

While I agree with the gamble on the part of the prosecution not to have Rodney King testify, my guess—and it is just that, pure speculation, because I have not seen the transcript and have no specific information as to what the prosecutor did in an attempt to prevent what transpired—my guess is that the jury attached considerable importance to the fact that King did not take the stand. That is where the Fifth Amendment became a factor, albeit metaphorically.

It has been a commonplace among generations of legal scholars and court-watchers that invoking the privilege against self-incrimination can be accompanied by a high cost attached in the form of suspicion on the part of the citizenry in large that the Fifth Amendment was a legal cover for guilt. The courts have insisted that, while privilege is limited in scope and may be rendered moot by a grant of one or another form of immunity, the Fifth Amendment is a constitutional imperative, available to any citizen called to testify in a criminal proceeding at no cost to credibility or integrity. But that view is akin to a judge advising a jury to ignore something they have just heard in court.

Strictly, the Fifth Amendment privilege does not attach in the decision by the prosecution not to call Rodney King to the stand. In other words, the Fifth Amendment privilege was never invoked in the case. My point is metaphorical rather than narrowly legal.

In stark contrast to the fact that the person alleged by the prosecution to have been the victim did not take the stand to testify in his own behalf, to give his own version of events, the officers under indictment were familiar with courtroom procedures, reasonably articulate and forthcoming, clean-cut and professional in appearance and demeanor, and emphatic about the dangers of police work on the streets. The officers testified credibly to the jury in a jurisdiction where one of the salient values is to reside in a community which precludes such encounters, that police work often offends the sensibilities of ordinary citizens but the reality is that peace officers are doing their duty and nothing more questionable than protecting themselves.

The jury bought what it heard and saw and attached a cost to what had been denied them. In the balance, the jury came to attach less significance to the videotape than did those millions of us who had seen that tape again and again on television but did not have to sit in court day after day and consider other arguments.

I remain convinced, as I was when I heard the verdict read in the courtroom in Simi Valley, that the verdict was in error, misguided, indeed, preposterous, given the evidence on the tape. But I believe I now understand why the error was made, and I do not believe racism was an important factor.

3. Who Are Our Cops?

A profile of the local police recruit throughout the United States has emerged from the available data, and that profile has been replicated and corroborated by data gathered through every heuristical method: data gathered statistically and data gathered by means of case studies, data gathered through reactive measures and data gathered anecdotally, data gathered historically. Throughout our society, the local police recruit is male, early twenties, with a high school diploma or G.E.D. certificate, whose background includes family or friends who were policemen, and who joined a local department either due to a long-standing determination or the absence of any imagined practical alternative.

Data on the full range of in-service training programs throughout local police departments, while somewhat more varied than the recruiting profile in terms of the inferences prompted, has yielded a picture more remarkable for what has been ignored than for what has been included. The central motif of in-service training programs among local police departments is a combination of athletics and marksmanship, *e.g.*, an emphasis upon weight training for physical strength and conditioning together with making officers responsible for maintaining varying degrees of skill with weaponry by obliging them to qualify on the pistol range no less frequently than once every three months. Beyond that, in-service training amounts to a series of graduated demands which, when satisfied, can contribute to the likelihood if not insure promotion. The overwhelming emphasis throughout these promotion programs is administrative. To put it simply, the emphasis is upon learning to administer a local police department by and large in the fashion in which businesses are run.

To reiterate, what is truly remarkable about in-service training throughout local police departments in the United States is what those programs do not include. There is no pervasive or emphatic attention given to programmatic attempts to sophisticate police officers intellectually, socially, or in the law. For instance, a sophisticated awareness of search-and-seizure Fourth Amendment case law and its development as common law, or the same in a Fifth and Sixth Amendment convergence context of a Fourteenth Amendment due process clause context, arguably would enhance officers' skills in investigation, evidence, and reports to offices of district attorneys. Yet, such courses or programs are as rare and about as close to being regarded as fundamental to police training, at the academy level or in-service, as are courses on nutrition in medical schools.

Medical schools historically have discounted nutrition as subject matter because, paradigmatically, the profession has been and remains disease-oriented rather than health-conscious. Physicians are trained to diagnose and treat rather than to prevent disease.

A paradigm functions to channel the training of local police officers throughout the United States. The paradigm identifies three somewhat distinct and sometimes overlapping populations and trains cops to see each of these populations as composed of people opposed to efficient law enforcement. Consequently, police officers are trained by the very atmosphere of their work to see themselves alienated from the larger society they protect and serve.

As happens in instances of all paradigms, this pervasive image which directs police training was neither designed nor established by deliberate intellectual effort to do any such thing. Rather, the paradigm developed incrementally over time in consequence of historically arranged material circumstances until a unified and coherent image of one whole enterprise had emerged.

The first population identified is made up of lames, criminals, evil-doers. As one consequence of their training and the atmosphere surrounding their work day-today, police are likely to regard people suspected of criminal activity as morally defective individuals. Controlling crime is a high moral drama in which the policeman is a knight-errant slaying demons and questing for the grail. In this drama, so the paradigm has it, knights are seldom appreciated when there are no dragons immediately present in the forest.

Another population identified in the paradigm as opposed to efficient law enforcement is composed of people engaged in one or another form of lawyering. Police are trained to regard attorneys, judges, and everyone involved directly in the administration of formal adjudication as the enemy. These people are tiresome and dangerous. Their essential function is obstructionist in nature. Their work impedes, interrupts, delays what otherwise, *i.e.*, left to the police, would be swift and final law enforcement. To return to the knightly metaphor, attorneys, judges and their spawn may not be the actual dragons—suspected criminals, a somewhat redundant term in the paradigm, are the actual dragons—but they are nearly as bad unerringly because they insist upon hobbling the slaying by arcane and bizarre rules of chivalry which they invent, as though chivalric codes had any relevance when it comes to demons.

The third and last population identified in the police training paradigm, from whom police are encouraged by the very air they breathe to see themselves as alienated, is composed of the general citizenry, the public at large, in a word, civilians. To be sure, policing functions to protect and serve civilians but it is just there that the paradigm works to convey to police officers a fundamental lesson about their profession, namely, all civilians are potential suspects. Furthermore, the paradigm warns, civilians generally are unwilling, unable and unlikely to assist the police in their investigation and apprehension of criminals. Civilians want the police to protect them from demons but they do not wish to live in the forests where those demons can be found nor, in any place, do they wish to become involved in the slaying. Civilians are as likely to champion the rights of dragons as to praise and defend their knights, and this tendency becomes all the more pronounced on the part of civilians who have not themselves been victimized directly by demons, as in the adage that a liberal is someone who has yet to be mugged.

Whereas police officers function within a paradigm which instructs them to regard lawyers and judges as pains-in-the-ass, and actual criminal suspects as immoral defectives, the same paradigm encourages police officers to see the general citizenry as loose cannons, as an x-factor, an unknown element, unstable and unreliable and, on that account, dangerous. The rule for interacting with civilians is "Always civil, never polite." In that manner, "to serve and protect," while acknowledged, receives less credence than the single most salient principle of police work: "Trust no one but your partner. Suspect everyone."

Cops are taught that a civilian transforms himself—the world of discourse for police is chock-a-block with masculine metaphors—from a member of the population composed of the general citizenry into the population of lames or criminal suspects at the moment the civilian does not obey a civil command from a sworn peace officer. Once that transformation is underway, the police officer is trained to accomplish a single task straightaway, by whatever means the particular circumstances in which the transformation has occurred may dictate. That task is to control the suspect, to take the suspect into custody, in a formal and full-fledged arrest, an informal chat or conversation on a streetcorner or in an alley, or any degree of custody between those control polarities. The cop must arrange custody so as to be in control of the subject. Until that is accomplished, nothing else matters. Unless that is accomplished, law enforcement cannot proceed.

Seen as an event within the paradigm of police training, then, Rodney King was a large and powerful male who had attempted to avoid police custody in a high-speed pursuit. The suspect may have been perceived as more dangerous than that, *e.g.*, high on angel dust, driving under the influence, but no police officer would have understood Rodney King to have been less dangerous than that. The probability of that perception approaches the concept of inevitability on account of the salient features and the paradigm within which police training occurs throughout the United States.

When the Los Angeles police officers and officers from the California Highway Patrol finally stopped Rodney King's car, ordered him out of the vehicle, ordered him to assume the prone position face down and to place his hands behind his back, King did not respond immediately and entirely to the officers' commands. In the ensuing eighty-six seconds, Los Angeles police officers beat Rodney King fifty-one times with police-issue batons.

Preposterously, the jury acquitted all four indicted officers of all criminal violations save the one count against one of the defendants on which the jury was unable to reach any decision. In the wake of that verdict, substantial portions of the population of Los Angeles erupted, and the rage spread rapidly to cities across the nation: Seattle, Las Vegas, Pittsburgh, Philadelphia, Manhattan (NYC), Miami.

It seems patent that the verdict of the jury was erroneous because the videotape was evidence "beyond a reasonable doubt and to a moral certainty" of the guilt of the defendants. But it seems equally clear that questioning the verdict is no more compelling, no more important, no more productive, than questioning the source(s) of the police officers' behavior at the alleged crime scene.

The eruption of varying forms of social discontent in Los Angeles and other cities served to enshrine as orthodoxy what nearly all pre-verdict discussions of the King case had assumed, *viz.*, that the crux of the case was racism. Orthodoxy took the form of insisting tacitly that the four cops had beaten King because they were white and he was an African American.

A relatively few so-called conservatives throughout the United States argued against the orthodox position. They insisted that the police officers at the crime scene behaved as they had because it was a crime scene, *i.e.*, Rodney King was a criminal, a scofflaw, a denizen of the street underworld, and he got what such people should receive at the hands of police officers.

My view is that the behavior of the police officers, those four who were indicted for having beaten Rodney King and the other cops who were not indicted but who had been at the scene and took no effective action to prevent or to stop the beating, was highly probable on account of salient patterns in police training in Los Angeles, exacerbated by the Gates' administration of the L.A.P.D. but not different in kind from the basic motifs of police training throughout the United States.

Where is the groundswell of concern from the great American electorate about the recruitment and training of local police in our society? Is it any more difficult to understand that the recruitment and training of local police has as much impact upon their subsequent behavior as does recruitment and training in any other occupation or profession? It strikes me there are only two reasonable answers to that question: One is to suggest that the prevalent paradigm of recruitment and training of local police is correct. The general citizenry does not want to be informed or concerned with what goes on under cover of policing our society, at least not until our national conscience has been shocked and even then merely as lip-service and benediction rather than as nitty-gritty daily involvement.

The other response is to wonder how such an obvious issue as the recruitment and training of police can be overlooked by reasonably concerned and informed citizens. What power has served to hide that issue in plain sight?

4. Hoodlums, Hustlers, True Believers, and Their Victims

As a microcosm, CBS showed one block which had been burned out in southwest Los Angeles in the social rage which erupted in the wake of the jury verdict in the King case: an electronics store owned and operated by Iranian immigrants, an Hispanic bakery, a bookstore run by African Americans, a furniture store owned and operated by immigrants to the United States from South Korea.

In macrocosm, it has been possible to identify five populations who have interacted in Los Angeles and elsewhere in varying forms of social discontent as aftermath to the verdict: (1) One population has been composed of people who believe with all their hearts in the conventional wisdom that racism lay at the core of the King case. This population of true believers encompasses both genders, a wide range of ages, all racial and ethnic categories, a continuum of formal education and literacy running from lowest to highest, and a background of political perspectives including all conventional and radical positions and affiliations. (2) Another population has been composed of those who are always alert for opportunities in an urban setting to loot, burn, pillage, maim and kill, under color of a timely and highly charged atmosphere. These hoodlums, hustlers and thugs acted *en masse*, as is their custom. Urban police and fire services were overwhelmed by their numbers for a time. (3) Yet another population has been composed of the hapless victims: truck drivers and motorists pulled from their vehicles and beaten, robbed, or murdered by a mob; small business entrepreneurs attempting to realize the economic dream whose stores and companies were looted and torched; the people who had been employed in those stores and by those companies and are now without income; the residents of neighborhoods and communities who watched helplessly as their homes and possessions went up in smoke. (4) Still another population has been composed of civil servants who, in varying ways and under the aegis of various authorities, have attempted to restore order: cops, firefighters, mayors and their staffs, troopers from National Guard units and soldiers on active duty with the U.S. Army, governors, and one George Herbert Walker Bush. Particularly for the members of this population who were on the streets, they had to do their work while, simultaneously, defending themselves from the mobs of thugs and hustlers. (5) The largest population interacting with the others throughout the aftermath of the King jury verdict has been composed of all the rest of us, people who have not been touched directly and with the full immediacy of outrage or loss, people consigned by circumstance to the enviable yet arresting situation of appreciating what has happened vicariously and, in that sense, abstractly. Not only have we composed the largest population numerically but it may not be going too far to suggest that the extent to which and the specific ways in which social development in the context of the King case will proceed will depend in the largest part upon the nature of our involvement. In large measure, we shall influence the future in context on account of how and what we think and every other dimension of our praxis, day-to-day. With that in mind, I offer something about which to think:

A number of so-called spokespersons for conventional wisdom, prominent individuals such as Eleanor Holmes Norton, U.S. Congressional Delegate from the District of Columbia, have said repeatedly that the jury in the King case was all-white. In fact, the jury was composed along ethnic lines of ten whites, one Hispanic and one Asian. To be sure, there were no African Americans on the jury but neither were there any jurors living in an urban setting nor any who were poor.

Hypothetically, would Rodney King have been beaten had he been white? All other things being equal, hell yes! Suppose King had been white and the four cops African Americans. What then? *Ceterus paribus,* hell, yes! Suppose the jury had included several African American suburbanites who had attained occupational or professional standings sufficient to generate income and aspirations appropriate to residing in Simi Valley, Oxnard or Ventura. Would such a jury have acquitted the defendants? *Ceterus paribus*, hell, yes!

King would have been as likely to have been beaten had he been white, Hispanic, Asian or otherwise because King was beaten by cops and cops, by and large, are trained to beat any suspect in circumstances similar to those in which the hapless Rodney King found himself. They will do it because they have been trained to do it, trained to regard it as their work. If you do not believe suspects in similar circumstance should be beaten, you had better become informed about and involved in attempts to change the salient pattern of police recruitment and training.

The hypothetical jury would have been as likely to have been as wrong as the actual jury because the actual verdict had far more to do with an error by the California Court of Appeals in changing the venue to Ventura County than with racism. The verdict had far more to do with the prosecutor, exercising his professionally trained judgment, having decided not to have Rodney King testify than with racism. You had better become an informed court-watcher if you wish to become involved in attempts to enhance the process of formal adjudication.

What makes it seem so frequently to so many that the criminal justice system in the United States has a double standard, one norm of justice for whites and a very different norm for "Just Us," is composed of one part mythology and one part effectively disguised reality. The mythological dimension functions, as mythology always does, to attempt to actualize what values have ordered. When people believe deeply enough that something ought to be true and factual, they can develop mythology which works to bring about that alteration, more or less effectively. In the present instance, mythology centers on an attempt by people who do not have what they regard as their fair share of the American pie to get it. The reality effectively disguised, the second component in the image of a double standard in criminal process, is rooted in the development of American political economy and centers on the dialectic of surplus populations. I shall try to explain these components succinctly by taking them in turn.

Mythology: What Criminal Process Does Not Consider

Presently, nationwide, one in every four African American males between the ages of eighteen and twenty-six is involved in the criminal justice system as an inmate, on parole or probation. In some jurisdictions, the data indicates even higher rates. In the District of Columbia, for example, 42% of young African American males are in the criminal justice system: incarcerated, paroled from having been incarcerated, on probation and liable to be incarcerated without further adjudication. Given that the most reliable statistics indicate that African American males are in varying degrees of custody within the criminal justice system at rates between one-fourth and nearly half the entire population, and that those rates contrast markedly with rates under ten percent for white males in the same age stratifications, it is not difficult to see the material circumstance which gives rise to the mythology.

Whereas the mythology focuses upon significantly higher rates of arrest, incarceration and sentencing for African Americans compared to whites, the criminal justice system does not pay any attention to those statistics. Indeed, when obliged by formal adjudicative procedure to consider such information, as in *McCleskey*, one criminal justice system argues that such statistically arranged comparisons are without meaning.

When the focus shifts to arrests, convictions, and sentences *per se* and away from rates *per se*, the comparison of mythology to fact changes. Now, criminal process emphasizes factual guilt whereas the mythology dismisses factual guilt and insists upon a focus on motivation. The mythology argues that what we ought to consider is why such large numbers of African American males engage in criminal activity, why they are arrested and incarcerated in such large numbers, and why they receive significantly longer or harsher sentences. The actual focus in criminal process is upon factual guilt itself. Social circumstances and motivation are given much less credence.

To elucidate, consider that an argument has persisted between prosecutors and defense attorneys in criminal law over the extent and the ways in which criminal process has been stacked in favor of the prosecution. While that argument can be intriguing, one point is conceded by both sides although defense attorneys are unlikely to admit the consensus in adjudicative contexts or other circumstances in which they feel such an admission might affect adjudication. The point is that by the time a criminal suspect has gone through the checkpoints of criminal process to have become a defendant, the probabilities of factual guilt are overwhelming. At that point, it has been not only the police in their passion for crime control who have identified the suspect as guilty but an intake team in a prosecutor's office has reviewed the evidence and determined not only evidence of factual guilt sufficient to sustain a preliminary hearing but sufficient evidence of legal guilt according to the canons of formal adjudication to permit taking the case to court. The operative passion in a prosecutor's office is not to get a conviction so much as to avoid making mistakes. Errors do occur, to be sure, but the system is stacked to make formal adjudication reliable and, in consequence of that stacking, the probabilities are that criminal defendants are guilty. The race of a defendant does not alter those probabilities. Alan Dershowitz's first rule of criminal procedure is, "Almost all criminal defendants are, in fact, guilty." His second rule is, "All criminal defense lawyers, prosecutors and judges understand and believe Rule I."

Reality Effectively Disguised: Surplus Populations

The fact is that the American political economy is threatened by the very surplus population it generates. "Surplus population" here is to be understood to refer to an aggregate composed of what the U.S. government will call "an acceptable level of unemployment," together with all those who are in fact unemployed but who are not counted in official statistics on unemployment compiled by the U.S. Department of Labor, and, by no means least, the "underclass" made up of sub-populations of people who are devoid, beyond their ability to change, of the means by which to enter the exchange of labor for wages.

As a political economy, post-industrial capitalism generates what has been termed "a reserve army of labor" as one means by which to keep the costs of labor low. It works this way: Since there are people out of work who want the jobs presently occupied by others, the supply of labor exceeds the demand, and wages, along with the costs of working conditions, can be maintained at minimal levels or, at the very least, at cost levels lower than would be the case if demand and supply were equal or if demand exceeded supply. The existence of this surplus, even when costs of maintenance are considered, is a positive asset to the political economy. Besides, the larger amount of the costs of maintaining the surplus at subsistence levels will be laid off in the form of uneven taxation rates to be paid by the upper echelons of the working class.

The trouble with all this is that, as the surplus grows larger, and particularly when social and political conditions change so as to lend increasing visibility to that growing surplus, the same population which the political economy generates as an asset also becomes a liability. For example, while the unemployed function in macrocosm to keep the costs of labor low, roving bands of increasing numbers of the homeless on the streets of American cities threaten the very political economy which has generated the conditions of homelessness.

The term by means of which to refer to a phenomenon which is both asset and liability, value and threat, is "dialectical." That dialectic is reflected in fact in the criminal justice system in the United States. The system functions to warehouse a substantial portion of the surplus, thereby maximizing and disguising the asset to political economy which that population represents and, simultaneously, reducing the threat.

In this analysis it becomes clear that the American criminal justice system is a result of the same material conditions which generated the rage and the eruption of social discontent in the aftermath of the verdict in the King case. There is no double standard in the criminal justice system. That system reflects a single, unified and historically generated standard, *viz.*, it is criminal to be poor in America. To be sure, racism in the United States exacerbates and disguises the crime of being poor by intensifying antagonisms among racial populations and individuals. But the root cause, thus, the arena for change, is political economy rather than race relations or civil rights.

At this writing, William Barr, Attorney General of the United States, has ordered a Justice Department investigation into the potential merits of federal indictments, not only against the four Los Angeles cops acquitted by the jury in Ventura County, but other peace officers, L.A.P.D. and C.H.P. alike, who were on the scene when Rodney King was beaten. The operative question for Justice Department attorneys will be whether King's civil rights have been violated by "intentional application of excessive force."

The possibility of federal indictments points at two considerations worth mentioning. One is that formal adjudication can work, albeit in a scope confined to matters legal. Due process includes a lengthy series of possibilities for review. While acquittals *per se* are not subject to review, so that federal judges can not second-guess the Ventura County jury, the federal judiciary may inquire as to whether federal statutes were violated.

A second consideration worth mentioning is that due process is a poor substitute or remedy for education, employment, and the full range of social institutions reflecting material circumstances which generate political economic productivity at micro and macro levels simultaneously. Racism is shameful and appalling. At its worst, racism colors and disguises an absence of opportunity for intellectual and professional development as though the lack was a matter of individualistic and institutionalized racial and ethnic antagonism.

George Will, a noted spokesperson for views taken generally to be conservative, has cited differing rates of children born out of wedlock as the essential issue in addressing social inequity: Among whites, the rate is 18%, among Hispanics 34%, and among African Americans 63%. Accepting those rates as accurate for the moment, the facts are that institutions and attitudes, in regard to parenting and childbirth or anything else, emerge from and develop appropriately to material circumstances. Change the material conditions which have generated unevenly distributed rates of illegitimate children among racial and ethnic populations and those rates will change. Change the material circumstances which have generated and maintained racism and racism will be alleviated, perhaps, eradicated. But effort directed at challenging racism itself, however well-intentioned and deeply felt such effort may be, will do very little to provide the parenting, schooling and jobs necessary to enable people to be productive politically and economically.

Perhaps, as has been suggested so frequently in the last two days, we have learned little in the years since the Watts' riots. Conventional wisdom assumes the essential lesson which has gone unlearned was given eloquent-because-genuine expression in the halting words of a terrified Rodney King during his first public statement since the jury verdict: ". . . Can't we get along? Can't we all get along?"

My view is that the essential lesson we have yet to learn, indeed, to notice, is that people anywhere do not get along so long as the material forces which generate their institutions and, in turn, their attitudes make it likely that their vested interests and ways of thinking about themselves will be antagonistic. Getting along becomes psychological and may be refined psychologically only once political economy has made it possible. Until African Americans, Hispanic Americans, Asian Americans, and European Americans lead lives day in and day out in which we all participate directly in the same social institutions, we shall continue not to get along. Like it or lump it. We shall not get along, even to the modest point of civility of learning not to kill one another, so long as the institutionalized patterns of our daily lives are exploitatively different.

There are few contrasts more stark than a comparison of southwest Los Angeles, even before the burning, and Simi Valley. Racial diversity is a mark of the former area whereas the latter is lily-white. The looting, burning and killing in southwest Los Angeles during the past few days ought to serve as sufficient evidence that racial diversity or homogeneity is not the operative question.

Too many educated Americans take it for granted that the Emancipation Proclamation, 1863, and the Fourteenth Amendment, 1868, together with the civil rights legislation during the second half of the twentieth century, have precluded apartheid in America. The reality is that we have developed a vigorous and resilient underground version hidden from view by our statutes and ideology. Like the South African variety, ours is a separation of peoples based in political economy expressed in terms of color. For all the enormous differences between the two nations, South Africa and the United States confront the same generic turning point in their histories: the population empowered by reason of capital, education and labor, will develop according to a fundamental mutuality of interests with the heretofore disenfranchised by opening to them the social institutions of empowerment, and those heretofore disenfranchised peoples will act in accord with that mutuality of interests by participating in the social patterns opened to them.

Dicta

Dialectics and Praxis in Baja

I had gone to Baja that summer to drink some beer and to sit in the shade and talk with Gaspar, a cabdriver in La Paz. We had met some years before and had taken to one another from the first. The trip had gone about as I had hoped. There had been good times, good talk and good beer. Together, Gaspar and I had gone to the Mexican World Series, held that year in La Paz, and he had arranged for a *gringo* to go with him to a sea turtle feast usually restricted to Indians.

Sometime during each of our outings I had tried to give Gaspar money, in amounts I knew were approximately what he would have charged any other tourist hanging about La Posada. Once or twice he had taken a part of what I had offered, just about enough to cover the cost of gas, but I was looking for some way to throw a bit of business his way and to do it so as not to injure pride or friendship.

It was August now and it had become very humid in La Paz. I asked Gaspar whether he would be interested in accompanying me to Cabo Son Lucas, the very tip of the Baja peninsula where the Sea of Cortez flows into the Pacific and there is always a breeze off the ocean. With dignity, Gaspar replied that he could not afford to take so much time from his work but that he would be pleased to drive me to Cabo and to arrange a room for me at the Sol Mar, the smallest of the hotels there and the only one which is truly Mexican in guest list as well as menu. I agreed, on condition that he would permit me to pay all the expenses we would incur on the way down and all that he would have on the drive bock to La Paz. It was agreed and we made our plans to leave in another day or so.

There was a small boy who spent much of his time on the outskirts of La Posada. He had skin the color of Mexican chocolate, thick black hair and eyes which seemed to dance. He did not smile all the time but, when he did, he lit up a place. He was about eight or nine and he had figured there was some chance of earning a peso now and again by being available to all the tourists who always wanted to do silly things and always had incredible amounts of money. Gaspar knew this boy, of course, and asked me if I had any objection to inviting the youngster to drive with us to Cabo and to rescue Gaspar from a solitary drive back to La Paz. I said I would be delighted to have the company of the young señor and, when Gaspar extended the invitation, the lad's grin could have powered the car during the trip. Gaspar went to the boy's home, a poor pescador's shack, and spoke with the mother who agreed to ask her husband for permission for the boy to make the journey on the following day.

Such particular affection between children and adult men is a thing one can see in Mexico. It is a proud thing, and true. It is a pattern which transcends variables of social class and income and is as marked between men and girls as between men and boys. It is a commonplace to see a Mexican family out for a stroll and to notice how the men are playing with and looking after the children, not as some onerous task which must be done but with real joy and passion. It is not that way in all other societies and it is wonderful to see. Gaspar could have invited any one of a dozen of his cronies but he wanted to spend his leisure time in the company of a small boy with dancing eyes and boundless curiosity.

In the morning, just after dawn, Gaspar and I drove to the boy's home to pick him up for the trip. Gaspar went inside and returned alone in no more than two or three minutes. As he slid behind the wheel he told me with much sadness that the boy's father had gotten very drunk the evening before and had come home in no condition for his wife to ask permission for the boy to accompany us. The father was asleep and, of course, the boy could not go with us without the explicit permission of his father. As Gaspar put the old Ford in gear and began to drive away, I saw the small boy standing just outside the shack. He was crying too hard to wave.

Gaspar was marvelous during the drive to Cabo. It was obvious that he wanted me to enjoy myself and to learn something more of Baja. He showed me the town where his parents had been born, a town built largely by a French mining company, and there at Triunfo we sat for a few minutes in silence in the cool of an exquisite old church. He showed me trees from which the Indians used to make arrows and other trees, the *ocote,* with which the telephone company made the gnarled and crooked poles which dotted the roadway. He teased me about *gringos* being silly enough to believe what he often told them, that it was the heat of the Baja sun which had made the telephone poles crooked.

At the time, both Gaspar and I were saddened by the little boy's absence. It was not merely that we had looked forward to the pleasure of his company but that we shared a sense of the boy's disappointment. As we sat in a cantina sipping beer just after we left the church at Triunfo, I told Gaspar that I thought the little boy had been dealt with unjustly by his mother and father, especially his father. Gaspar shrugged and said nothing until we were back in the car and had resumed our drive.

Gaspar's parents had been born in Baja and Gaspar had lived there all his life. He had left Baja exactly three times, twice when he had gone on the farm boat to Topolobompo and one other time when he had made the longest and most exciting trip of his life on the ferry to Puerto Vallarta. Gaspar knew little of the world outside Baja and almost nothing of the world outside Mexico, or so I thought.

He asked me why I thought what had happened to the small boy had been unjust. I said that the father had no right to get drunk and to be such a tyrant that his wife was afraid to awaken him to ask his permission for the boy to come with us. Gaspar said nothing for a moment and then he asked me to recall how often in recent weeks I had commented on the wonderful character of relationships between adult males and children in Mexico, how men were affectionate and loving with children, their own and the children of others. In this instance, I told Gaspar that the father had not behaved toward his young son with care or love and that I saw the father's behavior as contradicting adult male affection with children.

I have never forgotten Gaspar's response. "Amigo," he said, "that man is poor and he knows that his children and their children will be poor. He does what he can."

Part III

Voluntarism and Counsel: The Fifth and Sixth Amendments

Chapter Seven

Elementary Political Economy: Social Class and Racism

Prefatory Note

Four claims regarding the fundamental nature of the development of human social behavior were implicit in my, "Reflections on the Rodney King Case": (1) Material forces integral to the structure of historical circumstances set limits within which social institutions and, in turn, values develop. (2) Social class structure, established in historical contexts by material forces, fixes the probabilities of development for social institutions and, in turn, values. (3) The history of the United States reflects the impact of capital ownership and use as the basic material force which has set limits within which social class structure and, in turn, social institutions and values have developed. (4) Institutionalized racism, as a social institution which has been an integral feature of the history of the United States, is to be understood accurately as a consequence of capital and class structure, and not more than a proximate cause of other institutions and values.

Reaction to the Rodney King paper, on the part of students, colleagues at San Francisco State, police officers and attorneys and other practitioners in the criminal justice system, has called my attention to a need to explicate each of those claims. At the very least, the reaction has included a request that I clarify the claims, in other words, that if I do not write a book documenting each claim that, at least, I write shorter pieces to make explicit if succinct what I had left implicit in the previous work.

This excursion into elementary political economy is my initial response. While I do not imagine that I have included anything resembling a full treatment or explication, my aim has been to write a bit more clearly because more explicitly what I take for granted regarding the connection between class structure and racism.

I have been the principal beneficiary of an array of intriguing and productive conversations about the Rodney King case and my writing. Among the more important interactions, I am grateful to Professor Dwight Simpson, Department of International Relations, San Francisco State, who gave his insight and was generous enough to interview me on his KPFA-FM radio program (August 10, 1992); Professor Terry Diggs, Hastings College of Law, University of California, San Francisco, who was kind enough to write her impressions; Professor Devere Pentony, Department of International Relations, San Francisco State, who provided me with a number of insights both as regards the substance of the paper and its potential for publication; and Eric Beachum, a young African-American gentleman among my students who read my paper carefully and took the time to help me see more specifically than I would have otherwise what I needed to try to clarify.

I. An Analogy Regarding Structure

If it is not already a commonplace to point out that the United States has become a two-tiered society, surely such a suggestion can be regarded no longer as radical. However, when the nature of the tiers is taken to be fixed far more fundamentally by political economy then by racism, in other words, when the suggestion is that we are not a society segregated according to black and white except as one consequence if being divided according to rich and poor, the viewpoint remains both uncommon and radical. That is the view taken in this paper. Consider the following homely analogy.

The game of baseball has developed to a point where it is essential to designate every pitch not hit as either a ball or strike. Umpires call balls and strikes as an integral feature of the game. However, the game has many other dimensions as well and all of these, together with balls and strikes, amount to the aggregate of procedures and regulations that is the structure of the game as a whole.

Similarly, the United States has evolved as a society in which institutionalized racism is an integral feature of life, touching every individual directly, one way or another, day-to-day and trans-generationally. Racism is one among an array of social institutions which together reflect and reinforce the class structure of American society.

Racism is to social class as balls and strikes are to baseball. To analyze American society, in a context of any event or series of events, as though racism was the exclusive or even among the root causes is akin to imagining baseball as nothing more than a reflection of calling balls and strikes. Whether the object of analysis be the game of baseball or social change given the structure of society, it is the game or the structure *per se* which must be understood. When it is social change which one wishes to understand, one must begin by recognizing that the structure of the process emerges from material rather than ideational circumstances.

II. Capital as Force of Production

As a set of elements in the structure of human social behavior, ideational factors come in a variety of forms, for example, ideology, values, and basic assumptions. In these and other forms as well, ideational factors tell us about ourselves-in-the-world and about how things work. These are images, entities of the mind, and they function to make sense or nonsense of the world, to provide insights into the daily behavior and the collective character of the people of a society. They can explain the mundane and the banal as well as the complex and esoteric Without them, all would be madness.

Yet, for all their significance, ideational factors are overrated and otherwise misconstrued more often than not. Their genuine importance in developing human behavior can be understood accurately only by realizing that ideational factors reflect material circumstances rather than to cause those circumstances. Because they work to make sense of the more fundamental material conditions which give rise to them and within which they develop, ideational factors reinforce the more basic social motifs. In the limited sense of reinforcement, ideational factors may be regarded as proximate causes, but only in that restricted meaning of "cause." They do not cause social institutions. Ideational factors are akin to the wet pavement which results from a rain. Wet pavements do not cause rain.

For the development of human social behavior, the most fundamental or causally powerful material circumstance is whatever force history has enshrined to function at a particular time and place as the engine of productivity. To take one famous illustration, Marx characterized historical epochs as: (1) ancient, in which the force of production was slavery; (2) medieval, in which the force of production was land; and, (3) modern, in which the force of production became capital. It is less important to argue the extent to which Marx's outline was accurate than to consider the imagery as a view of historically-generated material forces of production.

The essential point to be understood is that, throughout the world for at least the last three hundred years, the fundamental force of production has been capital, its ownership and use. To understand any modern society with any quality resembling comprehensiveness and accuracy, it is essential to ask two questions in turn: In that society, what percent of the people own capital? What are the specific patterns according to which that capital is invested with the intention of generating additional capital? A materialist analysis begins with those questions, and analyses of any particular event or trends will be rooted in answers to those two questions.

Critics of materialist analyses insist that, for all the significance of capital in modern societies, it cannot be regarded as the only acceptable point of departure. Such critics are likely to see those engaged in materialist analysis as orthodox true-believers, ideologues of the Left. Four distinct, yet, related responses seem worth mentioning: (1) After all, there are substantive and procedural entities in the universe which function in precise ways and only in those ways. One can get vinegar from wine but not wine from vinegar. There is no such thing as a gene which functions apart from an environment. To understand such phenomena accurately, there is a sense in which it is necessary to become orthodox, although the term seems inappropriate in context. (2) Materialist analysis of human behavior lays claim to the entire empirical tradition of science. At bottom, admittedly, empiricism is a faith like any other in kind, that is, empiricism requires that one accept as an article of faith that matter is the fundamental reality, and that non-material reality, whatever the extent of its importance, must be understood as emerging from more basic material sources. (3) The consequences of materialist analysis, in any context, are distinguishable from, yet, connected to that analysis-as-approach. Those consequences, contextually, are subject to comparison with the results achieved by any and all other approaches. Within limits established by historical development of the hegemonic, beliefs which for most people in any society will be regarded without scrutiny as simple statements of the way things are, intellectual inquiry is a free-market enterprise. (4) A materialist focus upon capital, its ownership and use, permits us to see that the modern world is an outgrowth of an aggregate history which has included congresses, committees, and individual despots and geniuses riding horseback, but which has included as well a great many more instances of the ordinary and most frequently unrecorded events and lives of human social history. Steinbeck in his *Log from the Sea of Cortez* put it this way: "None of it is important or all of it is." In that aggregate process, all of which has been human experience while a scintilla has been driven by logic, the ownership and use of capital has emerged world-wide as the very definition of productivity. As such, capital has structured modern societies into those who own and use it and those who do not have it.

III. Social Class Structure

In the United States, as the final decade of the twentieth century has opened, the number of people who own and use capital as such is somewhere between one-half of one percent and three percent of the total population. Yet, that numerically tiny fraction of the world owns something like sixty percent of the total wealth of the United States. In order to understand accurately the meaning of this inverse proportion between population and wealth, three considerations are essential:

One consideration deals with the reliability of the data. Particular studies, using various criteria and methods, have yielded distinct results. But, while the data relative to particular studies may differ, what may be thought of as the big picture has emerged from all studies. Essentially, it is an image of the United States in which a small fraction of the population own and use a share well in excess of half the total wealth of the nation.

In view of the credibility of that essential image, another consideration touches upon the basic material condition of the tiny minority who own and use capital. First, it is a condition established historically and nomothetically, *i.e.*, it pertains to a population as such rather than to individual members of the population as such and the generativity has far more to do with momentum than with initiative or other individualistic characteristics. Second, the condition itself is that the population exerts a degree of influence upon the development of the whole nation far in excess of the number of persons in that population. The condition conveys extraordinary power.

A final consideration is the limit of that power. To put it most starkly, the power of the capital-owning population amounts to influence rather than control. The power is extraordinary because it is exercised by so few, but they do not dictate nor does their power determine the development of the nation. Although many critics of materialist analysis insist upon misconstruing an historical dialectic as a conspiracy, and while it hardly can be denied that advocates of materialist analysis have been known to engage in conspiracy theories, it remains true that notions of conspiratorial control by capitalists not merely are not inherent in materialist analysis but are antagonistic to that analysis. It is an error to imagine that anything in materialist analysis suggests that capital ownership and use conveys an exemption from the dialectical development of history. Avoiding that error is essential to an accurate appreciation of what the eminent British historian, J.P. Thompson, has termed the "relational" nature of social class.

Capital investment as a process requires the purchase of labor, and the investment logic of the process makes it likely that labor will be perceived as a cost to be kept as low as possible. For its part, in turn, labor will be perceived by wage-workers as their essential means of engaging in social productivity and their aim will be to keep wages as high as possible. Thus, an historical and structural antagonism, as distinct from anything individualistic or as a matter of mere perception, marks the essential relationship between capital and labor. Historical development occurs in consequence of that relationship *per se* and will continue to be played in dynamic contexts of social institutions and values which come into being and flourish or wither within material limits established by that relationship.

In the United States, for example, people who do not own and use capital either work for wages or become more and more marginal. That is the essential material condition of labor as a social class and it has been imposed by the same historical development which has conveyed extraordinary influence upon the tiny numerical fraction who own and use capital. To reiterate, the relationship between capital and labor is historical rather than conspiratorial, nomothetic rather than individualistic, structural rather than *ad hoc*, antagonistic rather than tranquil.

IV. Labor and the Underclass

Societies seldom are bothered by logical inconsistencies in their ideologies. In the United States, for example, an ideology which includes an insistence upon classlessness has been placed cheek by jowl with notions of a sprawling and potent middle class. The tenacity with which conventional wisdom in America clings to the concept of the bourgeoisie and visions of social mobility is matched only by the perversity of those myths. We are immersed throughout our lives in social hierarchies while we profess to believe in equality. With regard to social mobility, the only reasonable inference to be drawn from empirical data about life and death in the United States reflects essentially the same image which may be taken from the data available on any modern society, and that is that the overwhelming number of people die in the same social class into which they were born.

As a social class, labor is arranged in a hierarchy, in the same fashion generically as the bourgeoisie, in other words, hierarchies of power arranged according to material resources. When wages at or near the top of the labor hierarchy are compared to those in the lower reaches of the totem, the comparison will seem to reinforce the conventional wisdom of a middle class district and the discrepancies can be glaring enough to prompt the erroneous image of a distinct social class beneath labor, *viz.*, the underclass.

A social class is defined or bounded by material circumstances historically imposed upon populations. To be sure, probabilities are high that distinctive sets of values will be associated with distinctive social classes. Market researchers seldom miss the point. Televised professional football commercial time is likely to be purchased to sell beer rather than wine, and automobiles in lower price ranges designed as imitation Ferarris rather than the genuine articles. But distinctive sets of values associated with distinctive social classes are consequences of material conditions which have identified and bounded those classes in the first place.

In the United States, the social class composed of wage-workers, *i.e.*, people without capital for whom the dominant motif of material exchange is their labor, without regard to the price from zero to sum which their labor may attract, be they judges, politicians or managers of industry at the top, unskilled laborers near the bottom or second and third-generation welfare recipients, mental clinic outpatients, misdemeanor and felony offenders incarcerated or on the streets and other unemployable rabble at the very bottom, has been defined and bounded historically by a generic material condition imposed by what they do not own and what they must endure as a consequence, *viz.*, wage-work. From bottom to top, labor as a social class is locked historically in a relationship with capital as a social class. The relationship is both productive and antagonistic and social development, whatever its direction, is the outcome.

V. Institutionalized Racism

The structure of social classes, in the United States, for example, the relationship between capital and labor, defines the game of social change, its probabilities, limits, and mechanisms. When racism, whether considered in the institutionalized sense or ideationally as a set of images and attitudes, is taken to be a root cause of social disorder, a serious error in analysis has been made. The agony of America in the wake of the jury verdict in the Rodney King case and the subsequent outbreak of violence in cities and communities across the nation is a case in point.

The error can result in a further mistake of taking what is in fact historical, structural and systemic for something to which cosmetic remedies may be applied *ad hoc*. One of the more important intellectual benefits of materialist analysis is that it yields a clear view of causal forces and conditions distinct from circumstances which have resulted from those causes. Prescriptions must work upon the illness and not merely upon symptoms.

Institutionalized racism emerged and grew to virulence in the United States because, in specific and developing historical circumstances in which it assumed epidemic proportions, racism suited the productivity and class structure of American capitalism. As is true with any social institution which persists over time, slavery in the history of the United States was a complex phenomenon. Nonetheless, to argue that slavery, in its most fundamental character as a social institution, was not primarily political-economic would be to argue against the overwhelming testimony of empirical data as well as to give an entirely new meaning to the historiographic doctrines of historical relativism. The plague of institutionalized racism since the Emancipation Proclamation demands no less rigorous a materialist approach.

Using that approach, institutionalized racism takes on a material character from which its ideational dimensions emerge. Racism is accounted for in terms of political economy more fundamentally than social psychology.

Essentially, racism provides surplus populations composed of the poor among various racial and ethnic minorities. A surplus population amounts to a reserve of labor which serves to keep the costs of wage-work low by creating the condition of a buyers' market, *i.e.*, more potential workers than jobs. As a matter of political economy, a labor reserve generated by racism shares a material condition common among all surplus populations, by whatever institutions they may have been produced.

In the United States, surplus populations include those generated by institutionalized ageism, which has disenfranchised the elderly poor; institutionalized sexism, which has provided a labor reserve of uneducated and impoverished women consigned in all likelihood when employed at all to relatively low-paying work; and criminalization, used to increase or decrease as material circumstances recommend the surplus population of the poor warehoused by the criminal justice system. The common denominator among all surplus populations in a capital-oriented political economy is poverty, and poverty in the fullest sense of the term rather than narrow notions of income level. Racism is no exception.

Yet, surplus populations are tricky. While their existence is a benefit to the political economy, when material and ideational factors increase the visibility of a reserve, or when their number becomes too large and maintenance too costly, surplus populations can threaten the stability of the very political economy which has generated them.

In the United States at present, the enormous productivity of our political economy is contradicted by increasing numbers of the homeless on the streets and in the doorways of every city, impoverished drug addicts, poor people who are among the HIV-positive, the poor who are mentally ill and left to roam willy-nilly among urban thugs, and the children and adolescents of urban ghettoes, indeed, the children of the poor writ large. We are a society marked by fabulous wealth in the hands of a very few, by varying degrees of material comfort enjoyed by a larger number and, as well, by urban infrastructures near collapse, uneven rates of infant mortality especially high among the urban poor, a health care system which all but precludes the neediest poor, inner-city and rural poor schools qualitative light years removed from suburban public schools, not to mention the private schools for the children of the rich, a welfare system which enhances the probabilities of dependence to a point where it may be regarded fairly as a plantation system, and a criminal process which pressures the poor systematically to waive due process guarantees by pleading guilty. Given the reality of those contradictions, materialist analysis predicts that, increasingly, larger and larger numbers of surplus populations will be brought within the sweep of our criminal justice system, our health and welfare system, and an emphasis upon dumbing our public schools at all levels by paying attention to training more so than education.

VI. Social Change

Understood as a process in the context of materialist analysis, social change is explained as proceeding from within material limits, while ideational factors play catch-up. During any historical epoch, under the sway of any particular force of production, social change will occur as a political-economic structure manages whatever accomodations may be required as responses to institutional threats to material structural stability. The acid test of any predicted social change, in materialist analysis, is its accuracy rather than whether or to what extent one advocates some particular development. Predicting social change is social science, not mythology.

Direct assaults on material stability, exemplified by the violence in south central Los Angeles in the wake of the Simi Valley jury verdict, are far more likely to prompt direct entrenchment and force in kind than progressive adaptation and change. To enhance the probabilities of genuinely adaptive social change, it is necessary to understand and attempt to influence political-economic structure.

Whatever satisfaction may be taken from pay-back, whatever degree of justice may be served by retribution, however exhilarating it may be to vent one's spleen as it were, attacking a political economy through violent civil disorder will prove counterproductive. That prediction has much less to do with the relative merits of one's case than with the generic nature of social change, like it or lump it.

What the United States needs urgently is less preaching and more learning. We have evolved as a nation to a point where we now confront an historical turning-point, one which offers fantastic opportunities and enormous risks, but a point on which we shall turn one way or another. Presently, we are too frequently constrained to regard ideational factors as direct pathways to social change. As they say in the South, that dog don't hunt.

Item

Early on the morning of the first court day following the verdict in Ventura County, an attorney who had been serving as privately retained defense counsel in a criminal case telephoned the office of the assistant district attorney prosecuting that case to say that he would not be in court. What he said was, "I am not going into that racist court."

That case was being heard in San Francisco County. Defense counsel was an African-American. The assistant district attorney was a white woman. The judge was an Asian-American woman. The defendant was an African American male.

At this writing, no disposition in that case has been affected, nor has the defense attorney contacted the court. Both the court and the Bar Association are investigating.

When the judge asked the prosecutor to explain what defense counsel had meant by his cryptic remark, the A.D.A. replied, "I am not certain, Judge, but I took him to mean that all criminal courts in the United States had been tainted by the jury verdict in Simi Valley."

Analysis

Outrage can be a partial explanation for human behavior, individual or collective, but outrage does not constitute an exemption from the demands of civility. In a context where professional behavior is required, the absence of an exemption must be all the more compelling, not because anything in the circumstances may not have warranted outrage but because professional skill demands it.

Defense counsel abandoned his client in the midst of a criminal proceeding. Counsel was in contempt of the court. The Bar Association may suspend or terminate counsel's license to practice law. The court may order counsel into custody.

Not an iota of the agony of racism has been alleviated. Indeed, it is arguable that defense counsel has contributed to it, albeit unintentionally.

Item

> "We are motivated first and foremost by values."

George Herbert Walker Bush, President of the United States, in an address in Los Angeles, several days after the violence in the aftermath of the jury verdict in Simi Valley.

Analysis

This excerpt was taken out of context. Granted. In that context, the remark may be understood as: (a) a partial explanation of why the current national administration was not inclined "to throw money at the problem," (b) conventional political rhetoric, (c) a belief sincerely espoused about the nature of human behavior, (d) all of the above.

While the soundest answer to the foregoing multiple-choice undoubtedly is (d), simply because all of the first three choices are highly likely, the focus in this analysis will be on the third option. In his remark, an American President gave expression to one of the more deeply felt and pervasively held rubrics of American ideology, namely, that values as such are the primary motivating or causal forces generating human behavior. That same President had explained Desert Storm in similar terms, *i.e.*, the United States went into Iraq and Kuwait with military force in order to safeguard the ideals of political freedom first and foremost, and any considerations of oil reserves in the area were less significant.

In a materialist analysis, the foregoing amounts to idealized nonsense. Worse, it reflects a view of human development itself which is more likely to inhibit than to enhance acknowledgement of root causes of social problems. Accordingly, the violence in Los Angeles and the war in Iraq were consequences of conflicts in values, therefore, as soon as, but no sooner than people get their minds straight, our problems will disappear. Education, jobs or, for that matter, oil, are of relatively minor importance.

Chapter Eight

Commodification: Political Economy as a Source of Imagery

Consciousness is, therefore, from the very beginning a social product, and remains so as long as men exist at all.

—Marx & Engels, *The German Ideology,* in *Selected Works,* v.1, p.32.

High Recidivist Rates for Auto Theft and Rape

The man was tall, handsome, with impeccable academic credentials and an impressive publication record. In conventional political terms, his outlook was decidedly liberal.

The woman was brilliant, attractive, with degrees from two of the most prestigious universities in America. She considered herself a radical.

Both were single, emphatically heterosexual, and socially active. As colleagues, they ought to have gotten along well professionally and, perhaps, they might have found their way to one another's bedrooms. The fact was they despised one another. While their mutually intense distaste was at least as complicated as any human interaction, it seemed to have sprung from a single story the man enjoyed telling.

As a scholar, the man's specialization was the prison industry, although that was not a term he ever used because it smacked too much of economics whereas he regarded himself as a sociologist and he enjoyed a strong sense of the distinctiveness of his discipline combined with an appreciation that one ought never to cross disciplinary boundaries. He had a repertoire of many stories but one of his favorites was an explanation of recidivism generally and high rates of recidivism in certain criminal indices in particular. The story went that men who have been incarcerated have been deprived of such pleasures as driving high-priced sports cars and the sexual company of women so that, when they are let out of prison, it is likely that they will steal Porsches and rape women.

Every time the woman heard the man tell the story or heard it repeated by his many admirers, she grew more convinced that the man understood nothing. In her eyes the man became merely another chauvinist pig, not only because he told the story but because he persisted in telling it despite the fact that she had acquainted him forcefully with her critique. For his part, the man never quite understood the woman's objection nor her increasingly intense dislike. In time, he dismissed her as yet another troublesome broad not worth his time.

While the interaction of the man and the woman might illustrate any number of lessons, I use it here to call attention to only one, namely, that the woman's objection to the man's story was based in her insistence that women were not akin to sports cars or any other objects. In her politics, woman were not objects. Stealing an automobile was not analogous to rape.

II. Feminism as a View of Commodification

The feminist movement, as history, political economy, and social psychology, continues to develop in a complex manner. Reliable generalizations in the midst of such complexity are difficult to come by and sustain. Substantive disagreement over principles, insight and analysis, as well as politics *per se*, runs deeply throughout the movement. The vehemence of argument among dedicated feminists oftentimes is more visible and dramatic than their shared understandings, and such argument can run the gamut from the relatively innocuous to the most significant topics.

Still, there is a movement as such, an entity in reality to which we may refer as feminism, and an important aspect of what that means is that, despite complexities and internal strife, feminists reflect a perspective which can be discerned and defined, however difficult and with whatever limitations or qualifying phrases such definition may require. This limited essay attempts no such intellectually courageous task. Here, the intention is far more limited and less ambitious. It is to offer a single insight as at least part of the essence of feminism.

Whatever else may be agreed to and regardless of such disagreements as may arise, the argument here is that feminism *per se* has been and must continue to be arrayed adamantly in opposition to the commodification of women. Opposition to the commodification of women is not sufficient as a definition of feminism but it is necessary in order that the definition be reliable. Insistence upon the view that women are not objects but people, not commodities but persons who lay claim to each and every fundamental human right, is the bedrock of feminism.

When Anita Hill and Clarence Thomas were on parade during Thomas's confirmation hearings in the U.S. Senate, at least one issue became obvious: Who was telling the truth? Had a person nominated for lifetime appointment to the nation's ultimate judicial body engaged in sexual harassment of a subordinate? As occurs so frequently in public spectacles, responses to the question became a charade and large numbers of people were caught up and swayed by the burlesque. "We believe you, Anita" bumperstickers appeared all over the U.S. and the whole matter was reduced to a tawdry affair which denigrated everyone. But there was an underlying sentiment expressed by many people which did not garner anywhere near the attention it may have deserved: Even if Clarence Thomas had done everything Anita Hill alleged, so what? What, after all, was so bad about that? The practice of males making sexually assertive advances to women, and the related practice of men using their prerogatives in a male-dominated society, and employers taking advantage of employees, were as old as time. Any woman with sense expected such treatment and the more successful women were those who had learned either to enjoy it or at very least to use it to their own advantage. That was just the way the world worked, eh?

The feminist critique of such a view was rooted in opposition to the commodification of women while the view itself, whether expressed by men or women, was rooted in tacit acceptance of that commodification. Essentially, the anti-feminist sentiment asserted that history had defined women as objects for the gratification of males. The essence of the feminist view was that, to whatever extent and in whatever ways women may have been defined as objects for the gratification of men, sexually or otherwise, the development of human consciousness had proceeded to a point where that generic injustice must become a museum piece.

Question: What force(s) made the anti-feminist view prevalent? Why was it, what was it, that made feminist consciousness so obscure for so many? Was it that feminists read history correctly while their opponents read it badly or not at all? Was it that feminists were gifted with insight while chauvinists were damned without any? Was it that feminism had become politically correct and was obliged by that development to do battle with the forces of darkness? Was it merely another morality play in which good people were arrayed against evil-doers? Was it, perhaps, that chauvinists were simply stupid?

III. Love and Contract: A Distinction

Sometimes, when the answer to a question seems elusive, it can be helpful to offer a distinction and thereby suggest that the answer may be found by pursuing distinct implications. Consider the following distinction:

Arguably, the essential character of a contractual relationship lies in its limitations, whereas the essence of a loving relationship lies in its unconditional or unlimited arrangement. So, for instance, in *Black's Law Dictionary*, fifth edition, contract is defined as "an agreement between two or more persons which creates an obligation to do or not to do a particular thing." The emphasis is upon obligation(s) to a particular thing. The very nature of contract, whether written or implied, is just that sense of limitation, an obligation to do a particular thing rather than other things. By contrast, the love of parents for their children—notice, not the entirety of the parent-child relationship but the loving dimension of that relationship is characteristically unlimited, unconditional. Parents and their children will engage in contractual relationships, to be sure, but the essential quality of their loving dimension is that each party is entirely vulnerable to the other, without qualification or reservation. Romantic love, heterosexual or homosexual love, the love of one comrade for another, love among the members of a family, even the love a person may feel for a process, nation or culture, reflect the common denominator of love *per se*, namely, unconditionality.

To take another illustration, consider the prevalent human practice of keeping score. Bargaining is keeping score. George C. Homans developed one of the classic positions in the social sciences explicating human society in its elementary form as what happens when two or three people get together to influence one another, with the understanding that the essential nature of the interaction is an exchange, a matter of what one party must give in order to get what is wanted from another party. Exchange is keeping score. Keeping score is a limited relationship, by implication, a relationship in which the exchange of particular goods or services between two or more persons marks the boundaries of the relationship. Keeping score is contractual.

It is not going too far to suggest that a substantial amount of the difficulties people experience in our interactions stems from not appreciating accurately the nature and prevalence of contractual relations. When the obligations of a contract are not clear or are not understood clearly by one or more of the parties, or when a person imagines a relationship or some dimension of it to be love whereas the reality is keeping score, human interaction can deteriorate rapidly and profoundly.

Some years ago, in a paper on the relationship between cab drivers and their customers, Fred C. Davis characterized cabbies vis-a-vis fares as a "fleeting" relationship. The metaphor is apt not only in the context of Davis's study but as a means of characterizing the most frequent form of human social interaction. Love may be thought of as analogous to child-birth in that it occurs with relative infrequency despite its fundamental importance. Thus, nothing in the distinction offered here between love and contract can be regarded accurately as a denigration of either form of social interchange, but it remains the case that, except for such rare individuals as Mother Theresa in the streets of Delhi—and even there it is noteworthy that much of the saint's energies are devoted to wringing contractual terms, written or implied, from Indian authorities—people are occupied with contracts for a far greater portion of their lives than with loving relationships. But what has the distinction between love and contract to do with whatever may contribute to the prevalent obscurity of feminist consciousness regarding the commodification of women?

IV. Contract and Commodification

It is the very nature of a contract to encourage the parties to keep score. When people are engaged in keeping score it is the score which matters, the winning and the losing, profit and loss, debit and credit, success and failure, satisfaction and frustration. People construe entities in exchange as commodities due to the generic social arrangement in which they most frequently encounter one another. Whether the description of that arrangement is honorific, in which instance people will speak of productivity or practicality, or the description is pejorative, in which case the language will have to do with people using people, is mere semantics, the half-full, half-empty glass of water. The reality behind the semantics remains the same.

There is nothing inherently sinister in contractual relationships. If contract is distinct from love, if contract is not more important than love although far more prevalent, contractual human interaction has been productive and useful in achieving some of the most glorious of human manifestations. Michelangelo's Cistine ceiling, indeed, much of the art of the Italian Renaissance, did not occur except as an outcome of a contractual relationship with one or more bishops of Rome, or Florentine princes. Sexual gratification via heterosexual encounters is basic to the process of human biological reproduction. Governments which operate according to a contract with its citizenry, in which arrangement government functions within limitations upon its powers imposed by the rights of its citizens, thereby avoid tyranny and promote democracy.

The sinister issue of commodification arises, however, when the mutuality of contract is misconstrued as a one-way process. Governments which operate with no respect for rights of its citizens, thus, with no limits on its powers, are tyrannical. Tyrannical governments commodify citizens as subjects. When the sexual gratification of one party takes precedence over all other considerations, the interaction has been misconstrued as though it were a servo-system rather than a genuine interaction.

The essential point here is that, while obligations are entities to be exchanged according to the terms of a contract, the parties to that contract are not commodities. Contract *per se* exchanges obligations, not people. That is the conditionality as well as the mutuality of contract. When the inherent mutuality of contract is misconstrued as a one-way system, the relationship ceases to be contractual because it loses its conditionality.

The worker in a contractual relationship with the employer does not become the property of the employer. The child does not become the property of the parent when they function within a contractual dimension of their relationship. The citizen is not enslaved by the power of government so long as the relationship remains contractual. To reiterate, the essential characteristic of any contractual relationship lies in its conditionality, in the limited scope of its terms. Therein is the mutuality of contract.

Commodification is understood here to refer to a process of misconstruing contract not as a conditional mutuality but as an unlimited tyranny. Thus, commodification is not to be understood as an inherent consequence of contractual relationships. Rather, commodification subverts and effectively puts an end to contract. Commodification sweeps people into the category of objects to be exchanged contractually as obligations, as things, thereby effectively precluding or terminating a contractual relationship by eliminating mutual conditionality.

V. Contract and Capital Reproduction

The fundamental position advanced in this essay is that the political economy of reproducing capital establishes a material base consisting of class structure and social institutions, including institutionalized ideology, within which manifestations of alienated consciousness become not merely possible but highly probable. Commodification is one manifestation of that alienated consciousness and the commodification of women is but one instance of that manifestation. Thus, the answer to be found in this essay to the question of why feminist opposition to the commodification of women has escaped the understanding of so many well-meaning, intelligent and often educated people, male and female, is that the political economy of capital reproduction has generated, as one among its indeterminate, *i.e.*, probablistic consequences, this particular example of a subversive notion of contractual relations. The reader is encouraged to notice that, in this view, there is no suggestion of determinism, conspiracy nor condemnation. There is only history.

1. *Capital as Wealth*

Understood as the fundamental material process which generates probabilities of social development, capital and its reproduction amounts to the index or criterion of wealth. Capital has been the primary productive force throughout the world for at least the past two centuries. Capital formation and reproduction has emerged historically as the principal engine which drives an interactive social class structure consisting of those who own capital in one position and all those who do not own capital in a distinctively different position. Salient features of environment peculiar to particular societies mark those who do not own capital as a peasantry or a labor force, and development, agrarian or industrial, is reflected in stages such as pre- and post-industrial, decentralized and collective farming. But the generic process of social class structure has been and remains those who own the criterion of wealth distinct from while engaged symbiotically with those who work essentially because they do not own the criterion.

Synonymous with wealth, then, capital must be understood distinct from money. Money is merely one form of capital. Other forms include land and real estate, investment, the power to hire workers, and the broadest range of social influence manifest in government, higher education and the professions. Indeed, people who make the mistake of imagining that wealth is synonymous with money are very likely to be people who do not own and do not understand capital, its formation and reproduction.

As capital formation and reproduction generates a class structure, the same engine drives the probabilities of establishing, maintaining and reinforcing or, conversely, precluding, discouraging and repressing, particular patterns of social behavior. These patterns are the institutions of a society and, generically, they include such motifs as family, education, property, government, law, crime and criminal justice, medicine, welfare and the like. Social institutions develop with greater or less likelihood, more or less rapidly with more or less controversy, depending upon circumstances of geography and history but according to a generic criterion, namely, relative appropriateness to capital reproduction. Social institutions develop as rationalizations of capital. Appropriate to the stage of development, the institutions of a society will develop in more or less integrated, *i.e.*, coherent and systematic, fashion.

2. *Ideology as Institution*

Institutional development will include abstract as well as concrete rationalizations of capital, that is to say, the ideology of a society will be institutionalized as prescriptions for understanding the more overt patterns of behavior. The ideology of a society will be more or less systematic according to the stage of development of capital reproduction, but ideology *per se*, the beliefs of a whole people, will function as abstract reinforcement and enhancement of concrete and more overt motifs of social behavior. An important key to appreciating ideology is not to attempt to determine whether ideology is more or less important than other social institutions but to recognize ideology as a probabilistic outcome in abstraction of the same fundamental material process which sets limits to and fixes the probabilities of development of those other institutions, namely, capital reproduction. To put it differently, what must be understood is the process of material cause and indeterminate effect.

Another dimension of ideology essential to an accurate appraisal of social development lies in understanding the distinction and connection between individuals and populations. The solitary individual entirely apart from society is an empty abstraction. It has no material reality; there is no such thing except as an image. People exist only in societies; human behavior is never divorced from human society, except as an ideological institution. The hermit, for example, is a person whose definition of self is centered in separation to the extent possible from others and is therefore contingent upon a definition of others. Individuality in all forms is a social process. Individuality develops according to and as an indeterminate consequence of social institutions rather than as a cause of those institutions. To suggest that ideology is institutionalized means in part that the collective beliefs of a whole people constitute one source of individuality. The other principal source of individuality lies in the overt motifs, *i.e.*, institutions, of society. In order to appreciate individuality accurately in all its genuine significance, it is necessary to recognize that individuality is a development *in utero*, that it is as profoundly and fundamentally social in nature as the child learning from its parents or, for that matter, the learning process itself. The values and beliefs, the cherished and revered notions of individuals, emerge from and develop in accordance with probabilities established by the combination of overt and abstract patterns of social: behavior generated in turn as more or less appropriate to the political economy of capital reproduction and its class structure. Thus, the reality of individuality as a social process is another key to appreciating ideology. The key does not lie in attempting to determine whether the individual is more important than the group. Rather, what must be understood is the process of material cause and indeterminate effect.

3. *Ideology as Distortion of Reality*

Thirty years ago, Daniel Bell described ideology as a Coney Island mirror. A century before, Marx had characterized ideology as a disguise. The essential point in both bits of imagery is that ideology functions simultaneously to reveal and to distort social structure. The reason to pay close attention to ideology is in order to appreciate a whole people reflected in their collective beliefs, but, at the same time, to be careful because the reflection is not entirely accurate.

The explanation of why the reflection will be a distortion is not too complicated once it is understood that social institutions develop subordinately to political economy, *e.g.*, capital reproduction. The limits of institutional development are set and the probabilities within those limits established by capital reproduction and its class structure. Institutionalized patterns of social behavior are subservient to capital formation, not the other way around. Therefore, when the time and circumstances of capital reproduction recommend particular patterns of behavior, concrete and abstract, those are the patterns most likely to develop. A distorted image can become a more effective rationalization of capital formation than a more accurate abstraction and criterion is never reality or truth but enhancement of the political economy.

For example, wage labor is essential to capital reproduction. That labor is one of the principal costs of capital reproduction and, as such, the process dictates that costs be kept as low as possible concomitant with high productivity. But wage labor can also be drudgery. An assembly line can border on a violation of the Eighth Amendment, for example, but capital reproduction recommends that workers on the line be encouraged to produce and discouraged from complaining. The ideology of postponed gratification, the values of timeliness and attentiveness, the dictum of "a day's work for a day's pay," are examples of abstractions likely to develop not because they reflect the reality of the work but because they contribute to making the work more productive.

4. *Individualistic Voluntarism as Ideology*

The suffix "ism" in English is used to indicate that the word refers to a doctrine or fundamental belief espoused in distinction from and often in opposition to other doctrines on the same subject. Thus, Catholicism refers to a body of belief firmly held distinct from Protestantism, Judaism, Buddhism, and the like.

The term "individualism" refers to a belief which carries an array of implications and complications but which is rooted in a single and straightforward notion, *viz.*, that human societies are composed of individuals as such. This is not a belief in individuals as members of groups but individuals as such, individuals *per se*. The doctrine is predicated upon an image of the single and solitary person, surrounded to be sure by other such solitary figures but, at least in the abstract, a distinct entity. Human societies, the belief holds, consist of some numbers of those entities.

As the basic unit of society, according to individualism, this abstract solitary figure becomes the bedrock upon which all subsequent analyses must rest. For example, a political platform or agenda will be evaluated for the extent to which it upholds the primacy of the individual in its various programs, or, a proposal for a particular curriculum in education will be examined in order to determine the manner in which the courses and instruction will enhance development of the individual, or, a poet such as Walt Whitman will praise the individual, as in "One's-Self I Sing" from *Leaves of Grass*: "One's-Self I sing, a simple separate person."

Individualism is culturally relative, that is to say, distinct cultures can differ sharply with regard to the extent a belief in the primacy of the individual as such is incorporated into those particular value systems. Thus, historically, Chinese culture has not been marked by individualism whereas English culture has featured such a belief.

The United States, its history, culture and ideology, is to individualism as Rome is to the Vatican, Mecca to Islam. Whether one looks at the Founding Fathers (*e.g.* Madison, *Federalist* No.10; John Adams's letter to Jefferson on "*natural aristoi*") or contemporary sports (*e.g.* "Bo knows . . ."; Michael Jordan MVP), commerce (*e.g.* Lee Iaccoca) or commercials (*e.g.* ". . . the old-fashioned way, they earned it."), films (*e.g.* John Wayne, Clint Eastwood) or foreign policy (*e.g.* President Bush on Sadaam Hussein *vis*-a-*vis* the Saudi war). Americana and the history and ideology of the United States are permeated by a tacit belief and reverence for individualism. As prerequisite to any critical appraisal of individualism among people in the United States, one must attempt to grasp the fervor and prevalence of the doctrine as a fundamental tenant of American ideology.

To the extent that one gets a firm hold on the significance of individualism in the United States, and it is neither simple nor easy to do that, what one comes to understand is that, in the United States, very little if anything in day-to-day life *en masse*, and less in regard to formal or institutionalized contexts, e.g. law, politics, commerce, medicine, education, occurs untouched by individualism. The everyday activities of the family and the conduct of businesses small and galactic are shot through with belief in the primacy of the individual. If, according to critics of American individualism, the Horatio Alger mythology, Lincoln's log cabin and "any boy (anyone?) can grow up to be President" become increasingly difficult to swallow in light of empirical realities, the varieties of individualism (e.g. heroic or rugged, progressive) continue to be enshrined near the top of American ideology.

Put simply, individualism remains as one of the ways in which the world works, according to the beliefs of most Americans. Individualism is not exclusively an American story, but no accurate appraisal of institutions and behavior in the United States apart from consideration of individualism is possible.

In American ideology, individualism carries a corollary: Since the individual as such is the basic unit of society, it follows that social policies and institutions should adhere to and enhance the primacy of the individual and, in order to do so effectively—here is the corollary—it must be understood that the essential nature of the individual as such centers upon a capacity for making choices. Choice-making is the individual's engine, the power source which drives the individual through life. Though this faculty for decision-making is not a sufficient definition of the individual as such, the corollary to individualism holds the ability to choose among options as necessary to any complete definition.

In keeping with the basic doctrine of individualism, the corollary relies upon analyses at the highest levels of abstraction. Thus, the capacity to choose among alternatives is not expressed in terms of limits or constraints regarding the availability of alternatives. Rather, in the abstract, choice-making is regarded tacitly as an absolute capacity, unfettered by historical and social circumstance. In other words, adherents to the doctrine of individualism and its corollary are less likely to focus upon restraints on choosing freely and more likely to assume that choices are made freely because doing so is the very nature of the individual as such. For that reason, the corollary can be thought of as a doctrine of voluntary choice, *i.e*, voluntarism, and the complex institutionalized ideology may be referred to as individualistic voluntarism.

One of the major implications of individualistic voluntarism is that people are responsible for their actions. More accurately, the ideology takes it for granted that the individual is responsible for the consequences of the individual's behavior in as much as the essential nature of that behavior is voluntary. Examples abound!

The agonizingly complex issues of abortion are reduced most frequently by ideology to the language of choice, as though being pregnant and not wanting to carry the fetus to term was a circumstance for which the woman had volunteered. Bumper strips reading, "If you don't like it here, go back where you came from!" convey an ideology which takes it for granted that such populations as southeast Asian boat-people and Hispanics who cross the border illegally have emigrated to the United States voluntarily, and are capable of returning to their native lands in the same voluntary fashion. In criminal law in the United States, plea bargaining as an institution has been upheld as constitutional by the U.S. Supreme Court time and time again on the grounds that the individual defendant facing prosecutorial and judicial discretion regarding charges and sentencing can plead guilty "knowingly and voluntarily." Defense counsel does not direct or coerce the defendant regarding the plea, anymore than the prosecutor's power to manipulate the indictment is regarded by the courts as coercive; defense counsel merely instructs the client as to the options and the defendant enters the plea freely while in open court and is therefore accountable for the consequences of that plea.

5. Individualistic Voluntarism as a Source of Commodification

Individualistic voluntarism developed in the United States as a mainstay of American ideology less so because of any truth the doctrine may carry than because it proved enormously helpful as an abstract rationalization of capital reproduction. Indeed, the doctrine became important precisely because it was so largely untrue, because of the particular ways in which it distorted reality.

The implication in the doctrine which was most valuable to the political economy of capital reproduction was the image of social mobility. Getting ahead in life was to be understood, according to the doctrine, as a process driven by the choices made by the individual, by the extent to which the individual was willing to risk the self and by the wisdom of the individual's decisions. The doctrine rejected images of hierarchy and historically imposed necessities, not only despite the fact but precisely because, people were immersed in that history and surrounded throughout their lives by that hierarchy.

The doctrine preached a rugged and cut-throat view of the individual's relationship to others. In that individualistic sink-or-swim, success came to be appreciated as seizing initiative from others, taking advantage of one's opportunities presented in and through the vulnerability of others, exploiting the weakness of others. The doctrine did not go quite so far as to insist that success could come about only by the individual punishing others but it did imply that such punishments as circumstances might dictate were permissable in the interests of becoming successful. Over time, the doctrine hardened and became one of the most basic ways in which the overwhelming number of Americans defined themselves and understood their relationships. In the process, the doctrine had a considerable impact upon the sense Americans developed of their most frequent and pervasive social arrangement, namely, contract.

The impact perverted and subverted the understanding of contract by replacing conditional mutuality with individualistic gratification. Most history does not occur because of logical considerations but all of history matters. Little if any design went into the perversion of the image of contract but it happened on account of the value offered by an equally distorted image of society for the process of capital reproduction. In that light, commodification writ large and the commodification of women as an instance can be appreciated as distortions of reality which have become fundamental in America precisely because they are misleading.

Chapter Nine

Social Change and Social Class: An Evolutionary Approach

Preface

The youngster looked across the dining table at his grandfather and asked, "Gramps, how does it feel to be so old?" The elder replied, "Considering the alternative, Jimmy, it feels pretty good."

Many people imagine an array of factors to be relevant to analysis of the process of social change when, in fact, those variables exist nowhere except as abstractions in the minds of observers. The error is the same as young Jimmy made when he imagined that his grandfather faced each day with the option of being younger.

Introduced to a materialist view of social change, many people will find it a pessimistic appraisal. Their own approach to social change is normative, *i.e.*, value-oriented, and they regard their values tacitly as characteristics of the process they presume to understand. What they find downright disturbing about a materialist account of social change is far less a matter of a discrepancy between explanation and reality than between reality and preferences.

Any perspective will influence if not determine the problems which appear in an analysis of anything. When criminal process in the United States is seen from a crime control view, for example, the fundamental problems which appear are generic inefficiencies resulting from far too much emphasis upon formal adjudicative procedures whereas, when criminal process is approached from a due process view, the basic problems appear as unreliable consequences stemming from too much reliance upon informal, non-adjudicative fact-finding, and when the view is from a class analysis, the elementary problems are those generated historically by material inequity and reinforced by a prevalent refusal to attend to the impact of that inequity.

With more or less clarity, any perspective will include attention to the generic issue of remedy, *i.e.*, how to solve problems, how to fix conditions to improve the quality of life for those involved. Akin to the generation of problems, questions of remedies will be influenced by the particular perspective. A crime control perspective will recommend greater discretion and fewer restraints upon police, whereas a due process view will suggest greater care with formal adjudication and the presumption of innocence while a class analysis will prescribe a day-to-day praxis realistically enhanced by class consciousness.

When the object of study becomes social change itself, particular perspectives will denote distinctive problems and promote solutions peculiar to those problems.

Comparing and evaluating proposed remedies becomes fully intelligible only when those prescriptions are understood to have emerged from, in consequence of and within limits established by, the distinctive claims of particular perspectives. How to solve a precise problem is less fundamental a question than what conditions appear problematic.

Introduction: The Individual and Individuality in Social Change

Whether and to what extent is the individual as such a locus of social change?

At least two elementary considerations prompt the question when social change is analyzed in a context of materialist-historical argument: (1) Individualism and its corollary doctrine of voluntarism have developed historically to a point in time where they occupy a profound position within American ideology. The unified doctrine of individualistic voluntarism has become part of the American hegemonic, *i.e.*, that most deeply placed collection of tacit meanings and values according to which most people in our society explain how the world works and within which meanings most of us play out our lives day-to-day. Essentially, the doctrine informs us that individuals as such are the bedrock of human societies, and that the ability to make choices is the bottom line of individuality. Thus, nothing less profound than the deepest and most pervasive level of belief prompts the question of the manner in which the individual *per se* behaves as the atom of social change. (2) It is a logical question. Materialist-historical argument highlights the logic by begging the question. To argue that the essence of human behavior is that it is social, and that individuality as such emerges as a consequence of and within limits of probability established by social institutions which, in turn, have developed historically in consequence of and within limits established by forces and social relations of political-economic production, as materialist-historical analysis argues, is to make an intellectual claim about the very nature of the development of human behavior. Such a claim demands the fullest possible explanation, complete with the most careful organization and consideration of evidence. Short of that comprehensive analysis, such a claim requires, at very least, an account of the individual's role as such in the process of socio-historical development, *i.e.*, social change.

Adaptation: the Individual per se in the Process of Social Change

The anthropologist, Yehudi Cohen, has provided a succinct definition of the term "adaptation" as an approach to the study of human behavior: "When we speak about adaptation . . . we are concerned about adaptations that have been achieved by the species as a whole at a particular stage of evolution or by populations within the species. The adaptiveness of any individual or series of individuals is merely a reflection or a special case of the adaptation that has been achieved by the group of which he is a member. . . . An organism's adaptation is its relationship (*sic.*) to its habitat. Thus, the concept of adaptation is historical: when we say that a population is adapting we mean that it is altering its relationship to its milieu in order to make that milieu a more fit place in which to live or to make itself more fit to live in that milieu."[1]

According to this view, human behavior is regarded as an holistic phenomenon which inherently is: (1) evolutionary, (2) historical, and (3) manifest at the level of populations. Question: Is adaptation an individualistic approach to the study of human behavior? Answer: No. Question: Does adaptation account for the behavior of individuals *per se*? Answer: Yes, but that account understands individuals by reference to larger human wholes of populations or species, never the reverse. The real significance of individuality among *H. sapiens* can be appreciated only through a recognition of the causal force of whole populations and their social institutions which set limits within which individuality develops.

What is the significance of idividuality in the process of social change?

The very nature of fanaticism is that it precludes consideration of contrary sentiments. For example, to the extent that one is committed fanatically to the doctrine of individualism, one is unlikely seriously to consider adaptation as an approach to the study of human behavior. As regards fanaticism, the reverse is just as true. But if one resists whatever appeal fanaticism may hold in favor of an intellect not empty but open, it becomes possible to consider seriously arguments which run counter to conventional wisdom and even those which take issue with the hegemonic beliefs in a society. No single aspect of American ideology is embedded more profoundly in the hegemonic than individualism.

When the study of human behavior is approached from the view of adaptation, the individual does not disappear as a significant object of that study. Indeed, individuality must be encountered zestfully. As the anthropologist, Clifford Geertz, has put it: "We must, in short, descend into detail, past the misleading tags, past the metaphysical types, past the empty similarities to grasp firmly the essential character of not only the various cultures but the various sorts of individuals within each culture, if we wish to encounter humanity face to face."[2]

The adaptive capacity of *H. sapiens* equips the individual person to cope, more or less successfully, with the demands of environment. The same holds true in essence for all organisms, that is, the nature of the connection between the individual and its habitat is relational and interactive rather than static and one-way. But *H. sapi-*

---

1 *Man in Adaptation*, 3 vols., Y. Cohen (ed), (Aldine: 1968), v.I, 2.
2 Clifford Geertz, *The Interpretation of Cultures*, (Basic Books: 1973) 53.

ens, as the self-appointed designation suggests, is marked by symbolic intelligence. If that symbolic capacity is not unique among organic life, surely our species is marked profoundly by it. When symbolic intelligence is considered as essential to human adaptation, when our symbolic faculty actually is evaluated rather than merely enshrined because we have it, symbolic intelligence appears as a mixed blessing. We need to understand the costs as well as the benefits.

The principal benefit is that symbolic intelligence permits, indeed, promotes a generic coping which is both swift and agile. Our species is able to speed-read habitat and to enrich the interaction of organism and environment with imagery. Among *H. sapiens*, imagery has a reality not merely because we create it but because it is essential to coping with habitat. While our species is marked physiologically by such severe constraints as slow locomotion, poor vision, and vulnerability, the symbolic capacity of *H. sapiens* constitutes an enormous advantage in coping with environment. But the costs are high.

The most fundamental cost which our evolution has attached to human behavior may be understood as the down-side of the advantages we enjoy in consequence of our symbolic intelligence. The down-side is that, while our imagery enriches our interaction with environment, it makes us prone to error. As we speed-read and symbolize habitat, we impede our own reliability. More so and more rapidly than most if not all other species, *H. sapiens* complicates our interaction with environment by means of symbolic inventions, the overwhelming number of which inventions have no reality except as we afford them by means of still further symbolic inventions.

Our species-wide capacity for symbolic intelligence may be our crowning evolutionary achievement. In any case, symbolic intelligence is not an option among our species. Rather, it is an imperative, rendered by evolution. But all glory is fleeting, and we might do well to remind ourselves that uneasy lies the head which wears the crown.

While the species as a whole is crowned by symbolic intelligence, for good or ill, advantage and disadvantage, the individual human organ is the locus of that facility. The genuine significance of human individuality may be appreciated accordingly: The human individual copes with an environment which includes both a symbolic dimension and a material base which generates imagery. Coping strategies adopted by individuals run the entire range of cost and benefit attached by evolution to the development of the species as a whole. The difference lies in scale or, put another way, in the difference between questions of survival and extinction at the species level and questions of life and death at the level of the individual.

Praxis and "the hegemonic"

In aggregate and over time, day-to-day coping strategies give rise to values, *i.e.*, to ordinary meanings or, at least, to meanings which will be understood as ordinary by the people in a particular society. As values are found more or less successful as the terms of coping, over longer periods of time they are culled and codified into ideologies, in other words, values somewhat more generalizable, esoteric, and connected more intimately to dominant social institutions for which they serve as rationalizations. At the deepest and most profound level of the human symbolic environment, ". . . is a whole body of practices and expectations; our assignments of energy, our ordinary understanding of the nature of man and his world . . . a set of meanings and values which as they are experienced as practices appear as reciprocally confirming . . . a sense of reality for most people in a society, a sense of absolute because experienced beyond which it is very difficult for most members of the society to move, in most areas of their lives."[3] That is "the hegemonic."

Among the hegemonic values in the United States, no single belief is any more fundamental than individualism and its corollary, voluntarism. One implication of this dominance is that praxis, the day-to-day unity of thought and all other forms of behavior is likely to be influenced by individualistic voluntarism. It is all the more likely that, when praxis incorporates materialist analysis, one will be obliged to challenge the hegemonic generally and individualistic voluntarism as one particular.

It requires far less industriousness to float along with the current than to swim upstream. The limitation of the easier course is that one's options amount to running aground or going wherever the current leads.

A materialist analysis of social change will demand considerable work. All the more effort will have to be expended in the United States where that analysis will run afoul of a number of the hegemonic values and, even more fundamentally, will be confounded by social institutions. Materialist analysis will be regarded as pessimistic because it demands hard work and precludes quick fixes. The criminal justice system in the United States provides a useful example.

By definition, most people who become interested in criminal process are likely to approach the subject from one or another conventional perspective (*e.g.*, Packer's normative models) (*e.g.*, a functionalist appraisal of scarce resources and high caseload). Accordingly, they will discern and identify particular sets of conditions as basic problems of criminal process, and they will find a materialist analysis short on account of those problems *per se* either will not be addressed at all (e.g., too little emphasis upon victims' rights) or defined in a manner which precludes conventional solutions (e.g., too little emphasis upon the legal rights of individuals).

Proposing solutions to particular problems always is predicated upon an assumption that one has an accurate assessment of the actual function of the system or structure. Prescription assumes diagnosis.

3 Raymond Williams, *Problems in Materialism and Culture*, (Verso:1980) 38.

Social Change and Social Class: an Evolutionary Approach

Men make their own history, but they do not make it just as they please

"From a materialist perspective, what is the solution to these problems?" This basic question, in a variety of forms, can be anticipated whenever students are acquainted with the rudiments of materialist analysis. The question warrants an intelligent response for any number of reasons, among which and not least in importance are: (1) the assumption regarding the very nature of social change which is implicit nearly always in the question itself and the sociology of knowledge which prompted the question, and (2) the intellectual legitimacy of the question just as a matter of logical analysis, and (3) the extent to which a thoughtful response to the question will take the form of a strategic explanation of class analysis. Those reasons have prompted this essay, and it may prove useful to begin with a brief identification of what is to be understood here by the term "materialist" or "class" analysis.

A materialist analysis shares with general empiricism an assumption regarding the nature of reality, holding that matter is the fundamental stuff of existence. Matter can be appreciated through the senses; matter is tangible, thus, can lend itself to inter-subjective testing. Qualified in that manner as an article of faith, materialist analyses need not be endlessly relativistic and productive of little more than sets of opinions contrasted with other opinions. The same qualification often has generated an appearance of dogmatism and/or arrogance on the part of someone engaged in materialist analysis. While materialists hardly are exempt from the full range of human temperamental failings, arrogance and dogmatism among them, the materialist metaphysic that matter is the fundamental stuff of all existence is at work far more frequently than foibles of temper and personality when analysis appears to exude these vices. The fact is that a thoroughgoing belief in the elementarity of matter demands, more than it merely permits, an intellectual integrity about the nature of things and procedures by which proper inquiry into that nature must be carried on. To put it another way, the materialist metaphysic makes it difficult to avoid an epistemology or theory of knowledge consistent with that view of reality.

Such an epistemology holds that knowledge ultimately is whatever living organisms may acquire from their interaction with environment. Defined in that manner, knowledge may be coded and conveyed in DNA and/or culture, and the extent to which, and the precise ways in which, a particular species engages in each process of transmission will be one of the most significant watermarks of that species as such. If this sounds remarkably similar to basic evolutionary biology, that is precisely correct. It is tough for a materialist to escape a basically evolutionary view of the universe. One can be ignorant of biology, of course, but to have been exposed to biology, whether through formal or informal processes, then to reject the gist of evolution, is a highly unlikely eventuality, so much so as to be downright anomalous, perhaps.

The coding and transmission of knowledge in our own species, if not actually unique among living organisms, surely is highly unusual in the extent to which humans code and transmit knowledge socially. And it is enormously important to recall that incidence of error is one of the distinguishing features separating genetic from cultural knowledge. While cultural coding and transmission promotes all the advantages of rapidity and flexibility, it also prompts a high degree of error, and that mixed blessing has marked us indelibly as a species.

A materialist perspective on human history, therefore, will have to offer an account of erroneous information or false knowledge. The mere fact that large numbers of people have believed something to be true does not by itself oblige a materialist to regard that thing as true; it does prompt a materialist to inquire into what it has been in the social or cultural environment of those people which has led them to believe in the truth of that thing. In other words, a materialist analysis will not see human error as individualistic, will not blame error on its victims, will not assume that human error denotes defective humans. To repeat, a materialist epistemology regards knowledge, however it may be coded and conveyed, as a result of the interaction of organisms with environment. Whether that information be erroneous or reliable, false or true, incorrect or correct, it originated in an organic interaction in environment, in the very condition of living creatures. The central question about human knowledge, so largely transmitted through cultural processes, asks about connections between particular historical circumstances and particular populations. If intersubjective testing of material data can disclose a mistake in which large numbers of human beings have persisted over time, the intriguing question from a materialist perspective is what there has been in the cultural environment of those people which has promoted that error. Indeed, from a materialist perspective, the genuine intrigue is precisely the same regarding truth, *viz.*, what historical conditions prompted it?

A materialist analysis will not consider human knowledge individualistically because of the extent to which we are marked as a species by reliance upon socially coded and transmitted information. It is true to say that we are a social species rather than a species of individuals arranged into societies, and that human thought or knowledge is one of the characteristic behaviors of our social species rather than a process or activity distinct from our behavior. The solitary individual, that is to say, the mental picture of a single human being entirely separate from all other human beings, is a figment of our imagination and evidence of the power of human imagination to invent and persist in error. The solitary human individual is pure abstraction, without actual, living counterpart. Each of us is an individual, to be sure, but none of us is solitary in the sense that we exist completely divorced from others. Furthermore, our real individuality stems from our social being, not the other way around. Joan Smith has expressed it nicely in the following passage:

> The essence of human life is that it is social. In the absence of social organization, the individual could not exist. Further, that social organization has a history: it is shaped and contoured by what has gone before. Men and women come together in social units to produce and reproduce their lives and, in the process, the social relations within which they accomplish these aims. In doing so they also transform themselves. *How* they do that is by what is called a *mode of production*. . . .
>
> To start with the individual as the ultimate unit of analysis is to miss precisely what needs to be understood: it is to start with something that is abstracted from the very processes and relationships that define the individual as such. . . .
>
> Certainly this does not mean that the individual is predetermined. Obviously, the actor who creates society is an individual but only as he or she works in and through particular sets of social relationships. These relationships both shape the individual and set definite limits on what he or she can do.[4]

Homo sapiens is a social species whose relatively brief history has been rendered intriguingly complex less so by duration and numbers of organisms than by the uniquely high degree of reliance upon socially coded and transmitted information. Human thought is not distinct from human behavior; it is a fundamental characteristic of human behavior. Indeed, thought is sufficiently basic to human behavior as to pervade the full range of social organization and change among the species. What people think, for example, what they may take for granted regarding the nature of social change itself as well as the particular elements in their environment which seem to them to cry out for change and the particular remedies they will propose, always is a consequence of their historically derived condition.

For all its variety, that condition remains what it has been always: social organization for the purpose of sustaining and replicating human life, people arranged in social units attempting to secure food, shelter and whatever else circumstances may render necessary for life. The most primitive and essential activity on the part of any species is to continue living; the human species is no exception to that biology. That is the basis of the materialist view that the mode of production—the ways in which the social species organizes itself to produce life—is the fundamental indeterminate cause in the development of human society.[5] A materialist will consider a mode of production as composed of two overlapping elements: (1) *the forces* or *means* of production, by which to refer to the historically derived generative power of a particular productive mode, *e.g.*, hunting-gathering, slavery, land, capital; (2)

4 *Social Issues and the Social Order: the Contradictions of Capitalism,* (Winthrop Publishers, Cambridge, Mass. 1981), 266.

5 This analysis cannot be characterized accurately as economic determinism, for it is neither narrowly economic nor deterministic.

the *social relations* of production, by which to refer to the range of patterned interactions among the members of a society, viz., class structure.

Any particular means of production will generate a particular set of social relations of production: The force of hunting-gathering prompted a patriarchy predicated upon size and strength. As a means of production, slavery created a scheme of social relations in which there were slaveowners and slaves. A medieval mode of production included a complex set of social relations resulting from the ownership or non-ownership of land. For several centuries, the essential force of production throughout the world, has been capital. That force has generated a set of social relations based essentially in patterns of behavior between those who own capital and those who do not.

Capitalists, people whose basic material activity is made possible by their ownership of the means of production, exchange what they own for goods and services, noticeably the labor of others, which in turn is exchanged for increasing capital. Capitalists constitute a basic social class in the modern world, *viz.,* a population whose relationships with one another and with other populations stem from and are limited by their elementary material activity. As the British historian, E.P. Thompson, has expressed it, social class,

> is a fluency which evades analysis if we attempt to stop it dead at any given moment and anatomize its structure . . . The relationship must always be embodied in real people in a real context. The class experience is largely determined by the productive relations into which men are born or enter involuntarily.[6]

If we are to appreciate correctly the nature of capitalists as a social class we must recognize accurately the other social class generated by the force of capital, namely, labor or the working class. The "fluency" to which Thompson referred means that one cannot understand one class in a set of social relations without seeing it interactively vis-a-vis the other social class in that set.

Labor, or the working class, is a population whose basic material activity is predicated in the fact that they do not own the means of production. That labor as a social class must work for those who do own the means of production,-is a relational fact generated by the historically derived force of production itself. In a class context, labor is no more of an individualistic and voluntaristic activity than is capital.[7] Each of these basic patterns of material activity, along with all of the dimensions of human existence that activity makes probable, has been generated by the evolution or development of human societies to a point where capital has be-

6 *The Making of the English Working Class,* (Random House, 1963), 9.

7 It should be pointed out as well, though as a footnote rather than as a main point in the argument, that there has been no suggestion here of a conspiracy, a charge one hears so often in supposed refutation of a materialist analysis. An evolutionary and historical approach precludes any notion that some particular social class has designed and established conditions to oppress another. Neither capital nor labor is exempt from evolutionary and historical momentum.

come the dominant means of production. Just as capitalists enter the elementary act of production by contributing what they own, the working class begins by contributing what it owns, namely, its labor. That labor is exchanged for monies in the form of wages which in turn are exchanged for goods and services.

To reiterate, a materialist analysis of human behavior begins with recognition of the struggle to produce life as the most basic indeterminate cause of all other dimensions of human social existence. That struggle generates social organization as a mode of production in which some historically dominant force will generate in turn a particular set of social relations. Throughout the world for the past several centuries, that force increasingly has been capital and the resulting social relations have amounted to a class structure of capitalists and labor.

The basic historical realities of class structure and class position limit the probabilities of human social interaction. Class position in a particular class structure will make it more or less likely that one will receive a formal education, that one will aspire to some particular position, that one will earn some particular maximum income, that one will harbor some particular set of beliefs, that one will entertain some particular aspirations for one's children. In short, the basic historical realities of class position in a particular class structure will establish limits *(bestimmen)* for the development of all other social institutions, including ideology. Such in outline is the essential picture of human development and society which a materialist analysis brings to the task of understanding and explaining anything more particular about human behavior in a particular society at a particular point in time.

For example, the question with which this essay was begun: "From a materialist perspective, what is the solution to these problems?" As is true with any question, comment or thought, this question always is prompted from within some social context replete with implicit meanings and dominant assumptions among which it is likely in this particular case that the person asking the question has in mind, tacitly, a view of social change *per se.* From a materialist perspective, it is important to recognize the power of what Raymond Williams has termed, after Gramsci,[8] the hegemonic:

> It is in just this recognition of the wholeness of the process that the concept of "hegemony" goes beyond "ideology." What is decisive is not only the conscious system of ideas and beliefs, but the whole lived social process as practically organized by specific and dominant meanings and values.[9]
>
> That is why hegemony is not to be understood at the level of mere opinion or mere manipulation. It is a whole body of practices and expectations; our assign-

---

8 Antonio Gramsci wrote *Prison Notebooks* while in a Fascist prison, 1927 to 1935. See *Selections from the Prison Notebooks of Antonio Gramsci*, Q. Hoare & G.N. Smith (eds & trans)(International Publishers, New York: 1971).

9 Marxism and Literature, (Oxford University Press, 1977), 108–109.

> ments of energy, our ordinary understanding of the nature of man and of his world. It is a set of meanings and values which as they are experienced as practices appear as reciprocally confirming. It thus constitutes a sense of ideality for most people in a society, a sense of absolute because experienced reality beyond which it is very difficult for most members of the society to move, in most areas of their lives.[10]

The hegemonic in our own society includes within its system of meanings and values a particular view of the nature of social change. It is likely that the question with which this essay was begun will be asked from within that view: tacit, inchoate, absolute and reciprocally confirming, in short, what will pass for common sense in our society regarding the nature of social change. It is a view of social change which understands the process to be quite different, indeed, altogether different, from the understanding which a materialist perspective will afford. In comparison with a materialist analysis, common sense will regard social change as more mechanistic and voluntaristic than historical, more individualistic than social, and as having far less to do with social class than with such intangibles as will, desire, taste, sensitivity and conscience.

The dominant and common sense view of social change in our society is complex and varied but lends itself nonetheless to a basic characterization or description, one which Drew Humphries and David Greenberg have called "theories of agency," according to which, social rules,

> do not create themselves, but are instead the product of "entrepreneurs" who crusade for the adoption of the rules they wish to see enacted, perhaps at the expense of others . . . Theories of agency identify the social agents responsible for changes . . . and specify why they seek change.[11]

The authors made it explicit that theories of agency extend "to include group or collective entrepreneurs as well as individuals."

To put this in the most ordinary terms, the sort of terms in which theories of agency are most likely to be experienced as common sense, social change comes about in consequence of the actions of individuals by themselves and in concert with others. People see a problem which cries out for solution and they get together and solve it. The basic ingredients in the process of social change, according to this common sense, are individualistic recognition of circumstances in which things are not right and the energy to galvanize themselves and others to work at solving or rectifying those wrongs.

---

10 *Problems in Materialism and Culture*, (Verso Editions and NLB, London: 1980), 38.

11 "The Dialectics of Crime Control," *Crime and Capitalism*, D. Greenberg (ed), (Mayfield Publishing Company, Palo Alto, California, 1981), 211.

The entrepreneurial view of social chance suits the institutions of capitalist political economy and, as part of the hegemonic in such a society is no more surprising than other prevalent notions, such as, that government is a neutral arbiter of conflicts, that there is nothing but unbiased sweet reason revealed in the fact that the law will uphold the sanctity of contracts while unable to demand shelter for the homeless, that it makes sense for some fraction of the children of the working class to attend colleges and universities in order to get better jobs, that large numbers of people will see inordinately high rates of infant mortalities among certain communities as further evidence of the fact that some people cannot be helped, that nature and nature's law require that one is entitled only to what one can pay for, and that individualistic differences in temperament and personality are far more important in understanding human behavior than are variables of social class. As a material force, a capitalist political economy establishes limits within which social development occurs and within which some institutions including some beliefs become far more likely than others because they suit the material base from which development proceeds.

In sum, working class people surrounded all their lives by the facts of hierarchy and subordination are likely to believe in equality and social mobility, while capitalists are likely to see hierarchical organization and sound fiscal policy as among the clearest watermarks of a healthy society. The prevalent and tacit notions of each class are indeterminate consequences of the developmental limits set by the material base, namely, the mode of production. So it is hardly surprising that capital and labor embrace certain basic assumptions about human behavior and the nature of society, among which will be the entrepreneurial view of social change. It is necessary to recognize that the prevalence and institutionalization of those assumptions, among others, is a result of an historically derived political economy rather than a result of the accuracy, insight or wisdom of those assumptions. However, the institutionalization of belief is a fact of social structure which makes it difficult for most people in any society to consider seriously alternate views, and all the more difficult with regard to views predicated upon radically different assumptions.

Still, whether people in large numbers in our society are likely to recognize and admit it, there are intersubjective weaknesses to the entrepreneurial view of social change: (1) To take it for granted that individuality is the source of social organization rather than one result of society as such can be questioned by evidence drawn from the biological and social sciences. The probability that no amount or organization of such evidence will persuade many people that human individuals are not the ultimate atoms of human society is much less a consequence of any ambiguity or ineffective presentation of that evidence than of the reciprocally confirming interaction of material base and institutionalized beliefs. But, to repeat, it is clear from a materialist perspective that the realities of evolutionary biology and human historical development reveal individuality as a consequence rather than a cause of social organization, and that social organization proceeds indeterminately from a material base. (2) The entrepreneurial view of social change begs a series of questions regarding such fundamental matters as how particular individuals got to be powerful and influential entrepreneurs of change, and why it is that particular entrepreneurs see specific circumstances as demands for change, and how it happens that particular entrepreneurs will persuade others to support their causes for social change. (3) The entrepreneurial view of social change implies a voluntarism regarding human society which, while it is supported nicely by the assumption of individualism, is no more credible in light of intersubjective facts. The hoary notion that human circumstance always or nearly always reflect individualistic choices flies in the face of the overwhelming evidence of thc social sciences. Individual choice is an important aspect of human behavior which nothing in a materialist perspective denies, but it is an aspect which occurs in fact within limits established through historical momentum and social organization. Basically, the probabilities of individual choice are generated by class structure and class position.

To summarize, when the entrepreneurial view of social change is seen from a materialist perspective it appears to be individualistic, voluntaristic, and more psychological than historical. By contrast, a materialist account of social change begins with recognition of a specific though indeterminate cause, what Joan Smith has expressed as, "the way people go about producing the necessities of life—the goods and services of their society—is fundamental to explaining their problems as well as the institutions which surround them." Those ways are derived historically and, from a materialist framework, the derivative character of human behavior, *ipso facto,* is the vehicle for social change.

People who genuinely work to understand a materialist frame and come to the impression that the perspective is pessimistic in that it seems to deny or preclude social change, are likely to be people who have carried the assumptions of an entrepreneurial view into their work and, with such intellectual equipment, have tried to grasp the rudiments of a materialist sense of social change. That will not work. The assumptions of an entrepreneurial view must be put in abeyance at least long enough to consider a radically different perspective.

A materialist perspective does not deny social change while insisting that change always is historical, nor does the perspective deny the immediacy of social change. Rather, a materialist perspective insists upon social change as an inevitable and pervasive dimension of history and human behavior.

Historical momentum, the aggregate momentum of the past, generates particular productive forces and social relations within which particular institutions develop. People are born, live their lives, and die surrounded by those institutions. It is the very nature of human behavior that the highly normative patterns of a society are the limits within which individuality develops. By and large, people will believe what will be appropriate to their institutions, and as a result of where they stand in relation to those institutions.

In any human society at any point in its development, our own society currently being no exception, powerful forces are at work to maintain the *status quo* while other powerful forces operate to bring about change. Any condition in human society never is the consequence of one or the other of these forces but always of their interaction. Society is pulled simultaneously in opposing directions: stasis and change.

The simultaneity of continuity and change is a characteristic, a fundamental characteristic, of any evolutionary phenomenon from the simplest organism to the universe itself. The simultaneity generates tension between the two forces.

In human societies this tension is an historical consequence of people in various material circumstances producing their lives. While some people will see any particular aspect of the *status quo* as a bountiful and beneficial condition, others will regard that same circumstance as oppressive or as an impediment to progress. A materialist perspective makes it clear that these various perceptions or interpretations of one's interactions with environment are not merely psychological differences in perceptions as such, nor do they occur willy nilly and individualistically without pattern and social cause. These various meanings which people will attach to historically derived social conditions are consequences always of real people struggling amidst material institutions to distinguish those arrangements in their lives which produce bounty from those which impede and deny bounty. As people make those distinctions, they will strive to maintain the former and eradicate or alleviate the impact of the latter. The aggregate and collective consequence will be social change moving in particular directions.

Tension generated by the simultaneity of change and continuity can be appreciated at various levels of generalization: A person will reflect that tension in striving to both maintain and alter certain aspects of life as, for example, a parent who wants a child to be both a replication and an improvement upon the parental model. People in a society will understand their circumstances according to where their feet are planted in relation to their social institutions as, for example, a plant manager who places a premium on plant efficiency and an employee in that plant who is far more concerned with wages than productivity. The material condition of a society always is a consequence of the tension between limits historically imposed and a cause of social development as, for example, when the U.S. Supreme Court overturns a doctrine thereby prompting different law while reaffirming common law itself.

At whatever level of generality the tension of simultaneous continuity and change may be appreciated, one will be looking at the process of social change *per se.* Human behavior always is a consequence of that tension for the same fundamental reasons that our behavior always is social, namely, the reasons of our evolution. The tension resulting from basic contradictions is less something we have willed than an aspect of our historical being, and it is less accurate to regard the tension as problematic or pathological than as the developmental source of vital opportunities.

Human social behavior always is an historically derived consequence of material conditions and, simultaneously, a causal arbiter of development, an index of the future.

Whatever a materialist analysis of social change may lack in familiarity, ambitiousness and individualism it may compensate for by being realistic and accurate. The role of the individual in social change emerges from the material and social conditions of that person's life spent in the midst of a mode of production surrounded by institutions which have developed within limits established by those productive forces. Essentially, those limits are conveyed through a class structure and are manifest in a class position. A person is a reflection of historical forces as well as a factor in social change.

What a materialist analysis is likely to refer to as praxis, *viz.*, the unity of thought and all other forms of human behavior, means that every human act, including every thought, becomes a factor which works to sustain the *status quo* at the same time as it works to change it. Whether the behavior as a whole of any person impacts more for change than for stasis will be a matter of praxis, in other words, it will reflect that person's understanding of the world. Specifically, it will reflect the extent to which that person's class position is buoyed by class consciousness. The collective impact of praxis is, at once, human history and social change.

Dicta

The Warrior at the Bar

In an earlier age of the earth, the area which now lies at the southwestern base of Kilimanjaro was an enormous lake, a lake about the size of Manhattan. Amphibians, and creatures committed by evolution to either water or land, frequented the lake. Omnivores and carnivores, predators and prey, were sustained by its waters. Today, the lake is a dry and dusty bed of finely grained sand, a sand which is so nearly weightless as to resemble an abrasive facial powder.

That day we had spent about five hours on foot in the bush photographing game and recording their behavior. It had been marvelous, ranging from moments of fright through humor to poignancy. The time had been productive but it had been exhausting and now, as we sped across the dry lakebed of the Amboseli in a battered Land Rover, we were in pursuit of a bath, clean clothes, food and drink. The sand covered everything and swirled inside the Rover. We wore kerchiefs across our faces to keep the dust out of our eyes and nostrils. Only the driver expended any energy trying to see much of anything, and he really came closer to aiming the Rover than to driving it. He was aiming for the lodge, an old wooden building surrounded by a dozen smaller huts and lean-to's. The lodge in the Amboseli has some of the finest amenities in all East Africa, and the setting, in sight of Kilimanjaro, is magnificent.

As we arrived at the lodge late that afternoon around five, four of the five persons in our tired, dirty, and hungry and thirsty crew headed straight for their huts and a bath. As for me, I went for mother's milk, also straightaway. I headed for the small bar where I knew I would find a tall, nearly cold, dark brown bottle of dark African beer and, with little more on my mind, I stalked into the room while wiping some of the dust and dirt from my face with my kerchief. It was clear almost immediately as I entered the room that other locals and visitors had ideas similar to my own, though I was certain no one had a greater need, so I bellied up.

"Lager, if you please," I said, as the barman stood in the front of me, smiling a bit at the spectacle I must have presented. The beer materialized and as I put it to my lips with one hand, I put the kerchief in my back pocket with the other. That was when I saw him.

The bar itself was curved at one end. The other end abutted a wall separating the drinkers from the amateurs in the dining room and the outdoor patio areas beyond. Standing just at the curve in the bar so that he was to my left and facing me, was a Masaai warrior, dressed in traditional Masaai loincloth and burgundy blanket. He was the standard Masaai adolescent male, approximately twenty, about six-five. His musculature was stretched lean rather than enlarged. He had been groomed by one or more Masaai maidens, as was customary. His body had been rubbed with on oil which protected the skin and gave it a sheen not unlike bodybuilders preparing for a contest. His hair had been colored with a red clay and tied into tight ringlets. Next to him, resting against the bar, with the tip pointing toward the ceiling, was his spear, the only weapon the warrior carries into the bush, indeed, the only weapon as such the Masaai know. There he stood, about five feet from me.

Once the initial shock subsided, I told myself it was not surprising to find a warden having a beer at the local bar. The Masaai warriors are the wardens in the Amboseli, the only preserve in all of Africa where that is the case. Yet, for the same reason, it was surprising, for the Masaai are intensely and historically clannish and aloof. They go to great lengths to maintain and protect their ways from outsiders, from black and white Africans more so even than from Europeans, for that is where the greatest and most immediate threat lies. The Masaai refuse even to notice let alone to obey, local ordinances and governmental policies in whatever African nations they find themselves. They herd and tend their goats and cattle; they build their dung huts and move across Africa as the seasons tell them. Theirs is a good way, a proud way to be and, just for that, it was surprising to see a Masaai warrior standing at a bar drinking beer with Africans and Europeans.

But there he was, all the elegant, fierce aloofness of him, standing at the bar. He made no conversation, although that was to be expected since the Masaai speak a language quite distinct from Swahili and few are conversant in Swahili and many fewer in any other language. He did not smile nor offer any other particular animation. He stood, silently, sipping his beer.

In her classic study on the Masaai, Mirella Ricciardi accurately described the historical situation of the Masaai and the few other remaining traditional African tribes.

> . . . a whole way of life that's changing and slowly dying, to be replaced, for better or worse, by a Westernized civilization—abolishing tribal life and customs in favor of a more European civilization and culture, building schools and urging or obliging parents to have their children educated. Soon shorted and shirted Africans will replace the near naked man who for centuries has lived, and thrived or died, at the whim of nature.[1]

Try as they have and as they may, the Masaai are no more able to live without being influenced by their encounters with the social, political economic realities of East Africa than are Cubans, Russians, Albanians or Chinese able to live without being influenced by their encounters with the dominant worldwide material reality of capitalism. The Masaai cannot live apart from their environment any more than

1 *Vanishing Africa*, rev. ed., (1974) 10.

genes exist apart from environment, sociobiologists to the contrary notwithstanding.

The reality of the Masaai is not an image of the distinctiveness of their traditional culture, as an abstraction set apart from their habitat and its material history. Rather, the reality is Masaai culture as material social processes and institutions which are themselves the consequences of interaction with the material realities of the larger historical environment. The reality is not an image of Masaai warriors as abstractions rooted merely to other abstractions about quaint and exotic Masaai ceremonies. Rather, the reality is the ordinary and everyday social processes which happen to Masaai warriors, maidens, adults and children as they are born, tend their herds, build their domiciles and move across Africa, an Africa which is in the throes of historical continuity and change. To be sure, the solitary Masaai warrior protecting his people's herds on the slopes of Olmuti, is real. But so was the warrior at the bar, sipping his beer, cheek by jowl with non-Masaai Africans and Europeans.

Part IV

Criminal Justice and Social Justice

It is something to show that the consistency of a system requires a particular result, but it is not all. The life of the law has not been logic: it has been experience.

Oliver Wendell Holmes, *The Common Law* (1881).

. . . Nothing separated us but history.

James Carroll, *Prince of Peace* (1984)

. . . Poor whites, poor blacks and poor Hispanics now become illiterate together.

Jonathan Kozol, "Fatal Illiteracy" (1985).

Chapter Ten

Maps and Territories

People suffer class position and, far more often than not, do so without benefit of class consciousness. In a society such as ours, with its orthodox ideology of classlessness, class position without class consciousness will be all the more intensive and extensive. People will go through their lives as though the portion of a ship above the waterline was the ship as a whole. Not only will the larger number of those people fail to appreciate abstractions such as the principles of buoyancy; they will not understand accurately what they see all around them. Criminal process is a dramatic illustration.

Above the waterline, the superstructure of criminal process is an impressive and eye-catching display of competing ideologies and high stakes rigging. Consider Herbert Packer's notion of a normative antinomy at the heart of criminal process as case in point. Packer's supposedly antinomous ideologies of crime control and due process are significant and subversive.

The significance lies in the fact that Packer's models do represent sets of somewhat distinct and somewhat antagonistic values which mark criminal process in the United States. When former Chief Justice Warren Burger, dissenting in *Brewer v. Williams*, 430 U.S. 387 (1977), lamented that the corpse of an a eleven-year murder victim was excluded from evidence at trial of the confessed murderer because of the manner in which the police found the body, he captured accurately the gist of the suppression and the argument of the majority as well as the basic antagonism between emphasis upon crime control and due process values. While the Exclusionary Rule will be defended in a particular case and/or in general as a means by which to enhance the reliability of criminal process, it will be criticized as an obstacle in the path of the righteous and zealous attempt to repress criminal activity.

The subversion lies in the fact that Packer's models share a number of profound sentiments, although these are not the "common ground" which Packer suggested, and that the weight of these shared sentiments, buttressed by the supposed antinomy, in fact reinforces the *status quo* in the criminal justice system. Furthermore, the entire emphasis upon normative issues obscures the actual importance of material considerations by assuming that social institutions develop according to the beliefs and values of the people involved. It may well be that social institutions develop in consequence of material forces generated historically and that values and ideologies emerge and flower according to limits set by those institutions.

For clarity, it may prove helpful to consider an illustration of what Packer suggested as common ground between crime control and due process, accompanied by an illustration of what was misleading about the suggestion as well as an account of the actual shared sentiments and the manner in which the confusion tends to strengthen the reality of the status quo: While Packer cites a belief in equal enforcement and limited prosecution as common ground, neither value will be reflected in the actual operation of criminal process day to day so that consensus upon the values *per se* can be achieved only at levels of abstraction divorced from equality. While prosecutors and defense attorneys may concede that prosecution of the law ought to be limited by constitutional restraints, and while police officers as well as district attorneys will agree that investigation of alleged criminal activity must be conducted within constitutional limits, it is far less likely, in the context of investigation or adjudication of an actual case, that police will agree with D.A.'s or that prosecutors will agree with defense counsel regarding a specific allegation that such restraints were violated. The point is that what Packer cites as consensual values exist only in the thin air of high-level abstraction, whereas operational reality on the same points reflects conflict rather than consensus. In a word, Packer has idealized criminal process.

Indeed, idealization is one among several important attributes of Packer's models: He suggests that superstructure gives rise to hull and keel below the waterline, i.e., that values generate social institutions. Another actual feature common to crime control and due process models is that they promote a tendency toward a functionalist fallacy, in which consequences are treated as though they were causes. In the context of that fallacy, for example, an institution of criminal process such as plea bargaining will be explained on the basis of scarce resources and high caseload, whereas the reality of resources and load, in criminal justice as in other social systems in the United States, are reflections of material productivity, distinctions between public and private institutions, and the distribution of resources generated thereby. Given the nature of productivity in the United States, the criminal justice system is a public cost to be borne as a means necessary to warehousing a segment of surplus population. In that context, plea bargaining can be understood as an altogether likely development.

Yet another of the actual basic assumptions common to Packer's models is the notion, at once anti-intellectual and parochial, that all one needs to consider in order to understand criminal process is criminal process itself. One need not bother with history or political economy. Anthropology and sociology are ancillary at best, and the biological sciences extraneous. The specialized scope of the models begs such questions as the manner by which a doctrine of due process such as legal guilt is to be appreciated apart from familiarity with the history of abusive power on the part of the state, how rape and abortion in the context of criminal justice are to be understood apart from social psychological processes such as blaming the victim, how distribution of public resources are to be approached apart from political economy. If Parker is not opposed to interdisciplinary education, at very least there is nothing in his models to indicate he believes it is necessary.

In addition to idealization, functionalism, and a narrow, overly specialized scope, both of Packer's models reflect a basic assumption that individuals as such are the fundamental units of human societies, that individuals as such are creatures whose lives are determined largely by free choice, and that social institutions develop in accordance with those choices. As a single term by means of which to refer to this altogether conventional, indeed, orthodox sentiment in the United States, one might call it "individualistic voluntarism." Its role and significance in the operation of criminal process is enormous.

When the United States Supreme Court considered a petitioner's allegation that his confession had been beaten out of him by police and that his guilty plea had been coerced thereby, the court argued that, whatever the actual merits of the allegation of coercion, no one had coerced the defendant as he stood in open court to enter his plea (*McMann v. Richardson*, 397 U.S. 759, 1970). The underlying issue at law was the institution of plea bargaining, and one might cite virtually any decision by the U.S. Supreme Court in the context of plea bargaining by means of which to illustrate individualistic voluntarism. (For example, see: *U.S. v. Brady*, 397 U.S. 742, 1970; *Santobello v. New York*, 404 U.S. 257, 1971, *Bordenkircher v. Hayes*, 434 U.S. 357, 1973. Again and again, both in state and Federal cases on appeal, the court has reiterated its standard for judging the validity of a guilty plea and, thereby, at least in part, its test of plea bargaining itself, viz., the plea was entered "knowingly and voluntarily" or "intelligently and willingly" *(U.S. v. Jackson*, 390 U.S. 570, 1967).

The context of plea bargaining is merely an example. What is illustrated holds true for criminal process as a whole: While material realities of political economy set limits within which the institutions of criminal process develop (*e.g.*, plea bargaining) and the characteristics of criminal defendants as a population are marked as surplus, the ideology of the law and criminal process hides those realities behind the disguise of individualistic voluntarism, in which costume people are led to see themselves as individual instruments of free will negotiating with other individuals whose task it is to administer criminal process in order to guarantee legal rights which, again, are assumed to be individualistic. While the law works in an inherently conservative fashion to reinforce the *status quo*, warehousing a surplus population all the while raising the narrowest questions and maintaining its ideology of individualistic voluntarism as well as the illusion that the law is a force for radical social change, the values of crime control and due process, supposedly antinomous, in fact combine to strengthen social class inequities. Landmark decisions involving indigency, for example, (*Gideon v. Wainwright*, 372 U.S. 375, 1963), alter the operation of criminal process but leave the material realities of class poverty untouched.

The litmus test of any model is the extent to which it represents accurately what it purports to describe and/or explain. Proper evaluation of a model, as a map, hinges upon recognizing that the map is never synonymous with the territory and that the worth of the map is a matter of accuracy rather than advocacy. With that in mind, what do Packer's maps describe and how do they compare as representations of criminal process with a materialist, class-based map?

The due process map idealizes as it describes criminal process as something to be found only in two places, *viz.*, the ideology incorporated in law schools and taught through that curriculum as though it was not a story but *the* story regarding criminal process, and in formal, adjudicative ritual on display in our courts. In other words, the territory described in the due process map can be located only in ideology, which is after all what the map suggests as it describes territory which is normative, and in ceremony marking judicial process.

The crime control map describes with tolerable accuracy the day-to-day operation of criminal process, although it stops short of an explanation of the causes of the values and attitudes it describes. (The same can be observed about the due process map, that is, it offers no causal explanation for the rituals of formal adjudicative process or for the values which, according to the map, underlie those ceremonies.) Still, as a description of the attitudes on the part of working practitioners in the criminal justice system day in and day out, the crime control map is reasonably accurate.

To reiterate, both maps are idealized representations of the territory of criminal process, both maps encourage the fallacy of functionalism and the short-sightedness of an overly narrow focus and, finally, both maps reinforce an ideology of individualistic voluntarism and thereby strengthen the status quo. But the ideological and ceremonial territory described in the due process map is a mountainous region, full of jagged rocks, sheer precipice, and magnificent vistas, while the crime control map describes a flat and straightforward territory through which one can pass quickly and efficiently despite its dense population. Traversing the due process region requires esoteric and even arcane alpine skills, those skills involved intimately with formal adjudicative processes, whereas the crime control flatland suggests travellers moving along nicely while equipped with diligence, common sense and moral righteousness. The alpiner is encouraged to make reliable judgments while the flatlander is encouraged to proceed with utmost efficiency, speed and finality.

In comparison with either crime control or due process maps, the class justice map is cumbersome and inconvenient to carry. It is a extensive relief map in contrast to the easy-folding projections. The reason for the inconvenience is that the class justice map is an explanation rather than a mere description of criminal process, *i.e.*, it includes an account of causal forces rather than treating the territory as a given.

The class justice map describes a bleak landscape. The vistas here are gulag-like and unpleasant. Travel in such a land is less a matter of choice, much less, than of historical necessity, an historical necessity within which people do make their own destinies but not necessarily in any way they choose. The class justice map explains criminal process as one among many indeterminate outcomes of political economic forces. The particulars of criminal process are understood as actual results of time and circumstance, which results were made likely in the first place by historically generated means through which people produced their societies and themselves but, again, not in any way they wished.

The peoples who live in the territory represented in the class justice map are, most fundamentally, members of populations: a few managers, an army of workers to run things and a rabble composed of unproductive and counter-productive surplus folks warehoused in that landscape. By and large, all these populations are at odds with themselves even more profoundly than they are populations at war with one another because, while they lead their lives in the actual surroundings explained in the class justice map, they continue to travel while using the more convenient maps which describe more pleasant topographies of individualistic choice.

As if all this were not distasteful enough, the class justice map and the explanation of criminal process it incorporates does not enlighten anyone as to how the terrain might be improved and made more livable. The map explains an historical process without providing lessons as to how we might fix history, except in suggesting implicitly that people ought to adopt a relatively unambitious view of social change not because such a view is more pleasant but because it is more realistic.

Chapter Eleven

The Zone of Privacy and the Structure of Wealth

1. The Penumbra of Privacy

When, in its landmark opinion in *Boyd*[1] the U.S. Supreme Court sought to touch an historical document by means of which to underscore a connection between property and privacy, the choice was Lord Camden, in *Entick v. Carrington and Three Other King's Messengers* (1765):

> The great end for which men entered into society was to secure their property . . . No man can set his foot upon my ground without my license, but he is liable to an action though the damage be nothing . . .

Subsequent to their extended excerpt from Lord Camden's opinion, the court recognized the import of the issue they were to decide:

> The principles laid down in this opinion affect the very essence of constitutional liberty and security . . . they apply to all invasions on the part of the government and its employees of the sanctity of a man's home and the privacies of life. It is not the breaking of his doors, and the rummaging of his drawers, that constitutes the essence of the offence; but it is the invasion of his indefeasible right of personal security, personal liberty and private property, where that right has never been forfeited by his conviction of some public offence . . . Breaking into a house and opening boxes and drawers are circumstances of aggravation; but any forcible and compulsory extortion of a man's own testimony or of his private papers to be used as evidence to convict him of crime or to forfeit his goods, is within the condemnation of that judgment. In this regard the Fourth and Fifth Amendments run almost into each other.

In that language, amplified of course in the entirety of their holding, the court announced a convergence theory according to which the impact of the Fourth Amendment's guarantee against unreasonable searches and seizures linked inextricably with the Fifth Amendment privilege against self-incrimination was taken to be a zone of privacy, an invulnerable zone of privacy, between the state and the citizen. "No man can set his foot upon my ground . . ."

---

1 *Boyd v. United States*, 116 U.S.616 (1886).

The zone of privacy was located by the Court in the *Constitution* as a penumbra or implicit right. In *Boyd*, that finding was rooted in property law, *i.e.*, "No man can set his foot upon my ground" assumed that one had ground of one's own. That property emphasis in *Boyd* became the target of a revisionist view of the zone of privacy. That revision was given classic expression by Louis Brandeis in his dissent in *Olmstead*[2] and in an influential essay written for the *Harvard Law Review*.[3] The essence of Brandeis's view was that the zone of privacy was a fundamental guarantee of the *Constitution* rather than an implication based upon property law.

> . . . The view that a fundamental right to privacy exists, espoused in the famous article by Brandeis and Warren, was gaining acceptance. This concept was defined in terms of a basic right "to be left alone," rather than in terms of the technicalities of English property law.[4]

While there were a number of distinct edges to Brandeis's vision of the zone of privacy, surely one of the more significant was the implication that it was not necessary to be a property owner in order to claim constitutional protection. It did not take long for this rather radical notion to take effect and to be reflected in an array of case law: "Although Justice Brandeis had lost the battle in *Olmstead*, by the second half of the twentieth century he had won the war. The theory that his dissenting opinion espoused eventually became the official position of the Court."[5]

The emergence of Brandeis's view that the *Constitution* included by implication a fundamental right "to be left alone" was buttressed considerably by a corollary development in jurisprudence, *viz.* the rise to official legal doctrine of the selective approach to the incorporation of rights under the due process clause of the Fourteenth Amendment, *i.e.*, substantive due process. That doctrine was given classic expression by Benjamin Cardozo in *Palko*:

> . . . In these and other situations immunities that are valid as against the federal government by force of the specific pledges of particular amendments have been found to be implicit in the concept of ordered liberty, and thus, through the Fourteenth Amendment, become valid as against the states . . . There emerges the perception of a rationalizing principle which gives to discrete instances a proper order and coherence . . .[6]

The "concept of ordered liberty," as the basis for a judicial process of selective inclusion and exclusion of specific constitutional guarantees meant that the court was to rely upon penumbral rights *per se*. In opinions announced by such advocates

---

2 *Olmstead v. United States*, 277 U.S.438 (1928)
3 Warren & Brandeis, "The Right to Privacy," 4 *Harv. L. Rev.* 193 (1890).
4 "The Life and Times of *Boyd v. United States* (1886–1976)" 76 *Mich. L. Rev.* 184, 212 (1977).
5 *Ibid.*
6 *Palko v. Connecticut*, 320 U.S.319 (1937)

of substantive due process as Cardozo and Felix Frankfurter, the Court established its discretionary ability to read between the lines of the *Constitution*, as it were, and to find various penumbras put there by the Framers and to incorporate those rights as applicable in state courts as well as federal courts via the Fourteenth Amendment. Privacy was one of those penumbras.

> The security of one's privacy against arbitrary intrusion by the police—which is at the core of the Fourth Amendment—is basic to a free society. It is therefore implicit in "the concept of ordered liberty" and as such enforceable against the States through the Due Process Clause.[7]

Then there were the two landmark privacy penumbra decisions in cases which involved a right to dispense contraceptive information[8] and another which promoted the legal doctrine that a woman had a fundamental right to an abortion, at least during the first trimester pregnancy and with consent of her physician.[9] The anonymous author of the article on "The Life and Times of *Boyd* . . ." published in the University of Michigan *Law Review* in 1977, undoubtedly had both *Griswold* and *Roe* in mind when writing the remark that Brandeis had won the war. At this writing it seems worthy of note that the jurisprudence of privacy did not end with Roe. It continues to evolve as court-watchers and the passionate advocates of abortion-rights who battle their opponents attached with equal fervor to an anti-abortion platform await the latest in a series of cases involving those issues.

However, the present focus is not abortion but the jurisprudence of the penumbra of privacy upon which legal issues regarding abortion, as well as a legion of alternate issues, rest. To reiterate the main point, a jurisprudential doctrine has emerged in the United States in a context of constitutional decisions in criminal law, according to which a zone of privacy separating the legitimate interests of government from those of the citizen has been established. Development of that doctrine has gone from property law to fundamental right and from dissent to orthodoxy. But it is one thing to develop jurisprudence. It is quite a different matter to develop extra-legal social institutions.

Transition: From Jurisprudence to Political Economy

Because classlessness rather than social class structure is taught as conventional wisdom in the United States, it may be helpful to provide a transition by means of which to encourage the reader to move intellectually from consideration of the penumbra of privacy to the structure of wealth. With that in mind, then, consider the following commentary:

---

7 *Wolf v. Colorado*, 338 U.S.25 (1949).
8 *Griswold v. Connecticut,* 381 U.S.479 (1965).
9 *Roe v. Wade*, 410 U.S.113 (1973).

> At that moment, as if to underscore the poignancy of our exile, there was a rap on the door and an oh-so-Anglican clergyman, a canon of the cathedral, opened it.
>
> He was as tall and lean as those upper-class clerics with the best jobs always are. Though he was middle-aged, his face was boyish and his hair was closely cut . . .
>
> In his clerical collar and striped seersucker suit he looked like a chaplain of the British Raj, and I realized it had been glib sophistry to assert that little remained to separate Episcopalians and Roman Catholics. In that "little," revealed in meaningless details like the color of a priest's clothing, were buried millions of colonized and murdered people, many of them Irish and many Catholic. In that "little" was lost the distinction between the people who built the Cloisters and the people who clean it. Nothing separated us but history . . .[10]

The Structure of Wealth in the United States

Conventional wisdom is not merely a matter of acceptance. Its more important characteristic is that consensus so often is resilient, practically invulnerable to critical appraisal. That which is believed prevalently, in the larger number of instances by far, that which has been acquired informally and casually as ideology rather than by any formal process of education, is likely to be accepted as truth apart from critical analysis. When conventional wisdom is confronted by contrary views rooted in empirical data, the surest prediction is that convention will dismiss the opposing evidence, sometimes by means of a head-in-the-sand response and other times by impeaching the credibility of the opposition, *i.e.*, killing the messenger, whether through intellectually authentic argument or, as is more likely, by vague assertions couched esoterically which suggest that the unconventional view has resulted from faulty methodology or through the more direct approach of *ad nominem* attack.

A quarter century ago or thereabouts, a body of evidence and an image of the structure of wealth in the United States emerged in a series of published works. Illustrative of the earliest portions of this work were Kolko[11] and Domhoff[12] and, of the later portion, Quinney,[13] Duster,[14] and Rieman.[15] That evidence, and the image it warranted, were laid to rest by conventional wisdom.

---

10 James Carroll, *Prince of Peace*, (Morrissey St. Ltd., 1984).
11 Gabriel Kolko, *Wealth and Power in America: An Analysis of Social Class and Income Distribution*, (Praeger: 1962).
12 G. William Domhoff, *Who Rules America?* (Prentice-Hall: 1967).
13 Richard Quinney, *The Social Reality of Crime*, (Little, Brown: 1970); *Critique of Legal Order: Crime and Control in Capitalist Society*, (Little, Brown: 1973); *Class, State & Crime*, (McKay: 1977).
14 Troy Duster, *The Legislation of Morality: Law, Drugs and Moral Judgment*, (Free Press: 1970).
15 Jeffrey H. Rieman, *The Rich Get Richer and the Poor Get Prison*, (John Wiley & Sons: 1979, 1984).

But facts are resilient, too. Buried alive, facts are more likely to rise from the grave than to lie silently forever. Other published works, supplemented by a legion of independent studies, have incorporated the same fundamental image of the structure of wealth in the United States as that which was featured prominently in the earlier work by *Kolko, et. al.* The data which has become available during the last twenty-five or thirty years leaves little room for reasonable doubt that the radicals of the 1960's had it about right when they outlined the structure of wealth. Whatever implications were drawn from the outline are another matter but, as to the empirically sound basis for the image itself, there can be no serious argument.

In *Class, State & Crime*, Richard Quinney provided the following overview of social class structure in the United States:

Social Class	**% of Total Population**	**Generic Description**
capitalist	1.5	Those who own and control capital
bourgeoisie	18.5	Professional, middle management, and bureaucrats
working	80.0	Labor exchanged for wages.
	10%	Technical: teachers, nurses, medical technicians
	15%	Skilled: craftsmen, clerical, sales, operations, transport, industrial
	30%	Unskilled: industrial labor, service, office, sales, clerical
	15%	Reserve Army: unemployed
	10%	Underclass: the pauperized poor

The salient developments in social class structure since Quinney's estimate appeared have been: (1) a numerical decrease of capitalists to something approximating a third of the mid-seventies' population while the share of the total wealth of the United States controlled by this class increased from approximately half to sixty percent; (2) a variety of shifts among the bourgeoisie and distinctive ranks of labor which, in the aggregate, have amounted to a bottoming of the structure, *i.e.*, numerical decreases among upper echelons accompanied by numerical increases among lower levels, accompanied by a decrease in the share of the total wealth of the United States controlled by the working class from approximately half to forty percent; (3) a slight numerical increase of the reserve army of unemployed and a larger and more significant increase of the underclass.

Social Class	**% of Total Population: U.S.A.**		**% of Total Wealth: U.S.A.**	
	1975	**1990**	**1975**	**1990**
capitalist	1.5	.05	.50	.60
bourgeoisie	18.5	15.0		
working	80.0	84.5	.50	.40
technical	10.0	8.0		
skilled	15.0	13.0		
unskilled	30.0	32.0		
unemployed	15.0	18.0		
underclass	10.0	13.5		

To avoid misunderstanding these estimates of shifts in social class structure, a *caveat* may be important: What Quinney's estimate was aimed at in the mid-seventies, the current estimate incorporates, *viz*., the big picture. The data has been expressed in round numbers, and it is possible always to take issue with particular estimates and/or with the very structure by means of which the broad comparison has been conveyed.

The main point is that, while particular estimates vary in particulars, and while it is possible to question the terms in which the comparative information has been arranged, Quirney's use of the term "bourgeoisie," for example, there remains no serious argument over the image of social structure in the United States, and of the salient directions of numerical shifts within that structure which have taken place during the past fifteen or twenty years.

Conventional wisdom regarding classlessness and social mobility to the contrary notwithstanding, empirical evidence leaves no important doubt that the United States remains a class society. The main feature of class structure in the United States is a numerically-shrinking fraction of the total population who control well in excess of half the total wealth interacting with the overwhelming numerical majority who control significantly less than half of the total wealth. The criterion which determines class position *per se* is whether the person owns capital. With capital, one buys labor as an investment whereas, without capital, one works for wages. At the bottom of the structure are numerically-increasing populations composed of the unemployed and the unemployable. A remarkable phenomenon has occurred during the past fifteen years: At each of the absolute ends of the hierarchy, a numerical shift has marked the whole structure to such an extent that it threatens continuity and prompts a series of policies in response to that threat.

Nothing in the foregoing analysis has been intended to imply conspiracy. As a social class, capitalists are as subject to historical momentum as are those of us who work for wages. What E.P.Thompson termed the "relational" quality of social class as an index of social structure[16] means, among other considerations, that capitalists are not exempt from historical development. They do not sit atop social structure while directing it. Rather, capital interacts with labor and the populations within each class are subject historically to distinctive as well as shared patterns of development. To be sure, their fractional number and majority share of the total wealth provides capitalists with extraordinary power to influence the direction of that development, but history and class structure dictate that it remains power to influence rather than to control, momentum rather than conspiracy, class position rather than individualistic motivation.

The Impact of the Structure of Wealth upon the Penumbra of Privacy and Its Zone

Consider the following illustrations:

1. The data on white-collar crime leaves little room for doubt that differential sentencing based upon distinct categories of criminal convictions is a pervasive characteristic of our criminal justice system. The U.S. Bureau of Justice Statistics has found that while 60% of those convicted of white-collar crimes had been sentenced to jailterms, only 18% were sent to prison for more than a year. By comparison, violent offenders receive prison-terms of more than one year 39% of the time. When high-ranking employees of E.F. Hutton admitted their guilt in having defrauded approximately four hundred banks in a check-kiting scheme, not even the ringleaders went to jail. The corporation was ordered to reimburse the banks for the money stolen and to pay a fine of $750,000 to cover the government's cost in having had its attorneys and accountants break the case and prosecute it. Daniel Farber, Professor of Law at the University of Minnesota, reported a study done by the U.S. Sentencing

16 E.P.Thompson, *The Making of the English Working Class*, (Random House: 1963) 9.

Commission in which the salient conclusion was that "the system for sentencing corporations is in serious disrepair."

2. The term used increasingly is "the black underclass." In various contexts, the term is used to point at a widening gap between the numerical majority of African Americans who have entered the mainstream of life in the United States and an increasing number of have-nots. Approximately one third of African Americans live in poverty under a combination of temporary employment and welfare. Beneath that poverty are four to five million African Americans disenfranchised in inner cities in a cycle of the absence of employable resources, ignorance, welfare, drugs and crime.

   Patently, all the ugly and deleterious consequences of institutionalized racism have been important factors in the emergence and development of the black underclass. But it is no less true that, while the population is composed of African Americans, the term "underclass" refers to political economy far more fundamentally than to racism, even institutionalized racism, to say nothing of racism in any of its psychological or attitudinal contexts.

3. More than a third—about 38%—of all the poor in the United States are children. Data gathered from the U.S.Bureau of the Census, the Congressional Research Service, and the Children's Defense Fund, indicates that one of five under age 18 and one of four under age 6 live in poverty.

   Differential rates of infant mortality throughout the United States are associated directly with differential access to health care facilities. Medical care in the United States, for children and adults alike has become a two-tiered system: approximately one fifth of the hospital beds in the U.S. provide close to one half of the uncompensated hospital care.

4. Early in 1987, the California Department of Corrections released the following data, including a projection for 1991:

Year	Inmates
1983	35,892
1987	59,300
1991	94,950

In the United States during the 1980's, total prison population increased from 329,821 to 703,687. During 1989, federal and state prisons throughout the U.S. increased the number of beds by almost 60,000. California's Department of Corrections opened two new prisons to increase the number of beds by 2,200,

attempting to keep some sort of pace with the arrival of 250 new inmates every week.
Today, throughout the United States, there are more than a million people incarcerated in federal and state prisons. That number does not include jail populations. Prison population increases by approximately fifty thousand every year.

5. The appellate process in criminal law in the United States has been the locus of an array of landmark opinions. Some of these have been expressed eloquently, *e.g.*, Hugo Black writing for a unanimous U.S. Supreme Court in Gideon.[17] Some have been classic dissents. One thinks of Brandeis in *Olmstead*,[18] Black in *Betts*,[19] and John Marshall Harlan throughout the era of the Warren court. Not a few of the truly epic dissents have been rendered by lower level appellate courts, both state and federal. Here, one thinks of Judge Learned Hand. And there was Bazelon dissenting in *Decoster.*[20]

Whether it was due to inconsistency on the part of the defendant himself, or to one or more errors by court clerks, the fact remains that the spelling of Willie Decoster's family name appears in the appellate record variously, as Decoster, DeCoster. In any event, the man appeared before the United States Court of Appeals for the District of Columbia Circuit, the court many have referred to as the second highest in the nation. "In brief, the case centered on whether Decoster's conviction for armed robbery was obtained in violation of his right to effective assistance of counsel . . . The district court found that defense counsel's efforts did not deprive the defendant of effective assistance or, if they did, that no prejudice was shown . . . In reversing the district court, the panel (of the Court of Appeals for the D.C. Circuit) held that in cases of a failure to investigate, as occurred here according to the panel, the correct standard is to presume that the failure to investigate impaired the defense . . . The court of appeals *en banc* reversed the panel, but in a decision that reflected a badly split court . . . The opinion announcing the decision of the court stated that the accused must bear the initial burden of demonstrating a likelihood that counsel's inadequacy affected the outcome of the trial.'"[21]

To that judgment, Judge David Eazelon dissented. In writing dissent, Bazelon conveyed not only the arguable injustice done to Willie Decoster but the more pervasive second-class law delivered daily the poor.

> Willie Decoster was denied the effective assistance of counsel guaranteed by the Sixth Amendment because he could not afford to hire a competent and con-

17 *Gideon v. Wainwright*, 372 U.S.375 (1963)
18 *Olmstead v. United States*, 277 U.S.438 (1928)
19 *Betts v. Brady* 316 U.S. 455 (1942).
20 *United States v. Decoster*, 624 F.2d. 196 (1976).
21 R.J. Allen & R.B.Kuhns *Constitutional Criminal Procedure*, second edition, (Little, Brown: 1991), 237.

> scientious attorney. His plight is an indictment of our system of criminal justice, which promises "Equal Justice Under Law," but delivers only "Justice for Those Who Can Afford It." Though purporting to address the problem of effective assistance, the majority's decision ignores the sordid reality that the kind of slovenly, indifferent representation provided Willie Decoster is uniquely the fate allotted to the poor. Underlying the majority's antiseptic verbal formulations is a disturbing tolerance for a criminal justice system that consistently provides less protection and less dignity for the indigent . . .
>
> My colleagues fear that judicial "inquiry and standards (may) tear the fabric of our adversary system." *But for so very many indigent defendants, the adversary system is already in shreds (sic.)* . . .

Nowhere in all criminal case law in the United States can one find a more straightforward expression of the presumption of innocence in due process, nor any more searing indictment of two-tiered criminal justice. It may be well to point out that Judge Bazelon was no crackpot magistrate or lunatic radical.

The Zone of Privacy and the Structure of Wealth

The major social institutions of the U.S. have developed into a two-tiered society, *viz*., a numerical majority who participate daily and with varying rates of productivity in the mainstream, separated increasingly from a disenfranchised, alienated numerical minority of paupers. The two-tier image is reflected in such fundamental social institutions as wage-work, the family, education, medical and health care, the law, criminal process and criminal justice. The essential and generic characteristic of the population Quinney termed "the pauperized poor" is that they are devoid of resources which might allow them to participate productively in the mainstream. In other eras the population was referred to frequently as rabble, a collection of more or less distinguishable populations which a political economy had rendered as surplus.

Steeped as it is in doctrines of individualism, conventional wisdom views such people as defective individuals per se. Accordingly, the underclass and the lower ranks of the unemployed are not populations within social class structure but individuals who, for whatever idiosyncratic reasons, have chosen to deviate profoundly from mainstream American life.

By contrast, a materialist analysis of the pauperized poor, the rabble, the aggregate surplus, explains the population *per se* as having been generated by the political economy and as having developed to a scale and a visibility where the population now threatens the stability or, at least, the tranquility of the very system of productivity which generated it. That is a dialectical view, *i.e.*, historically-generated phenomena exhibiting contradictory functions.

Prognoses always reflect diagnoses. The conventional image of paupers in the United States, as defective individuals, is a very different picture from that taken of surplus populations by means of materialist analysis.

When paupers are seen conventionally, remedies reflect the assumptions of individualism and voluntarism, classlessness and social mobility and equality of opportunity which are the bedrock of orthodox social analysis in the United States. A range of encouraging programs aimed at individual paupers to abandon their counterproductive deviancy and to take hold of whatever helping hands mainstream society may extend are likely to mark conventional prognoses. It is altogether likely that stress will be laid upon motivation as a necessary prerequisite to behavioral change. "You can't help those who won't help themselves." This notion of motivation will serve in two ways: (1) It will rationalize whatever policies are forthcoming and provide a pseudo-explanation of low rates of success. (2) It will rationalize the absence of more costly and more aggressive programs. "You can't throw money at the problem."

When surplus populations are viewed from a materialist perspective, prognoses are more likely to take the form of empirically-based predictions than recommendations rooted in normative considerations. The materialist will insist that it is far more important to attempt to understand reality-based probabilities than it is to spend time worrying over preferences. Exponents of conventional wisdom will find this aspect of materialist analysis terribly pessimistic.

Generically, the materialist prediction will be that the squeaky wheel gets the grease, *i.e.*, to the extent that a surplus population comes to be perceived as a threat to social order, that population will be the object of a range of programs aimed at alleviating if not eradicating the threat. Therefore, the prediction will reflect an incremental rather than an epic view of social change *per se*. Various outcomes of social change will be understood to result from interaction between mainstream and surplus populations, in a context of historical momentum, rather than as the consequences stemming from control by one or the other force. "It is true that people make their future, but not in any way they wish."

The constitutional penumbra of privacy and the jurisprudence which has emerged in the forms of case law, statutory law, social policy and ideology, offer a useful context in which to compare conventional and materialist approaches to poverty. Convention will rely upon a recipe composed of about equal parts of cost/benefit analysis and an ideology of classlessness, social mobility, and equality. It is likely that conventional estimates will be couched normatively, as values. Herbert Packer's work on models of criminal process reflects that characteristic of convention:

> Another strand in the complex of attitudes underlying the Due Process Model is the idea—itself a shorthand statement for a complex of attitudes—of equality . . . Stated most starkly, the ideal of equality holds that "there can be no equal

> justice where the kind of trial a man gets depends on the amount of money he has."[22, 23]

By comparison, a materialist analysis of privacy will pay less attention than that given by convention to norms, in favor of emphasizing political economic institutions. With regard to any surplus population, the zone of privacy will be infinitesimal, for all practical purposes, non-existent, and the jurisprudence of the penumbral right of privacy will not change that reality. Expansion or contraction of the zone of privacy is neither individualistic nor a matter of social mobility. It reflects social stratification, more particularly, the position of a population in social hierarchy. Surplus populations are the very bottom, composed of the lowest echelons of the unemployed combined with the underclass of unemployables. As such, poverty in the United States may not be regarded always as criminal activity but it is a material condition likely to attract the attention of the law. The squeaky wheel may get the grease but that grease can slide people straight into jail.

---

22 Herbert Packer, *The Limits of the Criminal Sanction*, (Stanford Press: 1968), 168.
23 The excerpt as cited by Packer: *Griffin v. Illinois*, 351 U.S.12 (1956).

Chapter Twelve

Truth Dictates and Justice Demands

(Inscription above the entryway doors Tennessee Supreme Court, Nashville, Tennessee)

Why study law, and criminal law at that? Three answers occur which have little to do with the claptrap found customarily in the personal statements of people applying for admission to law school. One answer is, why not? The *juris doctor* in American society is an E-ticket. It is a doctorate with considerably more marketability than a Ph.D. and far wider range than that afforded by an M.D. Besides, the *J.D.* can be earned in a guaranteed three-year curriculum standard throughout the United States. Compare that with the indeterminate-sentence of academic degree programs in which an M. A. can require nearly three years and a Ph.D. six or seven.

One of my two surrogate sons earned his *J.D.* at Golden Gate University Law and passed the California Bar to take his first job teaching English in a college in Turkey. He now works for the United Nations as a refugee officer; he was stationed in Jerusalem and is now in Sarajevo. The *J.D.* was his ticket to adventure. It is unlikely that he will ever practice law as such.

The other side of this coin is the matter of practical alternatives. It is not as though one considered a profession equipped with realistic options to become anything else. Options really depend upon circumstances. One cannot vote oneself in a professional company and, when one considers class position at schools such as San Francisco State, real alternatives get clarified rapidly. The law is public and, because of its marketability, agencies are waiting in line to loan money to people willing to study law.

Another answer is that law is no less significant, if is not more so, than any other object of intellectual and professional attention. No persuasive evidence exists that law, as study or profession, makes one a better person, but, it can make one less wretched and does not make one any worse, necessarily. It can be argued that the impact of law prompts the most estimable norms of character and deportment. While it remains true that individuals in law who not only ought to know better but probably do behave reprehensibly, a more revealing issue is whether that is more true about law than medicine, academia, government or commerce. Conventional perceptions may not be reliable, based as they are likely to be on scant information gathered outside the profession.

A third answer is that the law *per se*, and criminal law particularly, is attached intricately to the more profound process of socio-historical development. Studying law can provide insight into the underlying process of social formation.

Admittedly, the author is a member of the choir on this issue. The law is the most exciting game in town, so much so that nothing is in second place. But that bias is based in the fact that law, inherently and generically, is a strategy for social control, thus, a reflection of what and who is meant to be controlled and by what means, in any society. While bias remains bias, it can be sound reasoning, eh?

At my university, a working class school where most students are the first members in their extended families to attend an institution of formal, higher education, I have had the honor and privilege of observing at close hand the development of undergraduates who have learned to take law seriously. My other surrogate son at this writing is about to graduate with honors from John F. Kennedy University Law, editor-in-chief of *Law Review* and first-in-class. He imagines himself in my debt. While he may have benefitted by our association, so have I, but it has been the institution of the law rather than any individual which has generated and channeled his maturation, and will continue doing so. To reiterate a major theme of this book, in any society, the patterns of behavior which become institutionalized are the stage on which and within which individuality in that society will be played.

Law is a strategy for social development. Sustained concentration and analysis of the former can lead to wisdom regarding the latter. No guarantees, but there are none anywhere. Yet, law reflects social process in the form of organized productivity, institutional patterns, and consequent ideology and individuality, somewhat more directly and dramatically than other avenues of intellect. This is no mere assertion or empty claim. Consider the topics of the essays in this book and the manner in which they elucidate, despite the author's shortcomings as a writer, the most basic social process in which society reproduces itself, not as mere duplication but as simultaneous continuity and variation. How is reasonableness determined in law, the criminal jurisprudence of the Fourth Amendment, for example, and how does that formula for reasonableness reflect and differ from reasonableness in society writ large? What does it mean in law to say that behavior is reliable only when it is voluntary, and does that hold for the larger society as well? What is the jurisprudential basis for a claim to assistance of counsel, and is that claim peculiar to law or is it similar to assistance of physician, for example? What does it mean in criminal procedure to treat a defendant as though he were innocent? Precisely, in operational terms, what does that mean, and what implications does that meaning have for our larger society?

What one learns from study and profession of law will always reflect the person, in part. If one sees nothing in law beyond professional and material comfort, one is more mechanic than artist but that, too, is no more true in law than elsewhere.

I recall when I was quite young and considering the whole frightening issue of career. Most of what took place did not occur by design, mine or anyone's, but some of it did. Vividly, I remember wanting to write novels, an Anglo-American epidemic among the young, but I was unable to become facile with plots. My efforts produced nothing beyond what had been contrived too obviously.

One afternoon, I read my first case-at-law. As most students, even in the social and behavioral sciences and humanities, I had gone through undergraduate work without ever having been exposed to an actual case in law. Professors had mentioned a few cases in passing during their lectures *Marbury* was one I recalled having been referred to in several courses, but I had never sat down and read a real case. I had never been asked to do it and, while I might have done it on my own initiative, the fact was that I had not. Anyway, that afternoon I happened upon the Slaughterhouse case in which the U.S. Supreme Court took its first opportunity to announce the meaning of the Fourteenth Amendment.

I recall my reaction, even after all these years. I was struck by the obscurity and complexity of the prose but more so by the discrepancy between the holding on the part of the Court and what I had learned about the history of the Civil War, the Civil War Amendments and the Fourteenth Amendment particularly. The discrepancy was enough to prompt me to investigate and I found myself reading cases in constitutional law. When I came across *Palko*, I was stunned. Even the Slaughterhouse holding had not been as bizarre and different from what I had been taught as what Cardozo wrote for the court in that Connecticut case. First, wrote Cardozo, neither the Fifth Amendment provision prohibiting double jeopardy in criminal procedure, nor the Bill of Rights in its entirety, attached to the states, Connecticut or any others. As if that had been a mere appetizer, Cardozo explicated "the concept of ordered liberty" as the formula for selective incorporation and the meaning of due process in a Fourteenth Amendment context. I had been enthralled throughout courses in philosophy and an untold number of references during my undergraduate years but I had never had the opportunity to consider any philosophical formula which had the intellectual excitement of ordered liberty in constitutional criminal jurisprudence: It put the court at large, on horseback.

I was hooked. The more I read, the more productive my activity became, driving me to read further in case law and analyses. Gradually, I began to see jurisprudential lines, patterns, motifs beneath the specific arguments. I began to recognize salient issues of social development reflected in those motifs. When I got to Holmes's *Common Law*, for the first time since St. Joseph's there was a rival to Sr. Mary Andrew for my intellect.

Since, no subject matter has excited and informed, challenged and satisfid me as the law. Readily, I acknowledge my bias: I cannot understand why so many well-meaning and erudite people miss the energy and excitement to be had in studying law, but I can offer an analogy:

Conventionally, people misconstrue jails and prisons as places filled, with what William Ryan has termed "The Different Ones" in his book, *Blaming the Victim*. These are, according to convention, individuals separated from human society by reason of their defects in character and conscience, sociopaths devoid of the wherewithal to engage in civil behavior. In fact, jails and prisons are ordinary places populated to overflowing for the most part with ordinary folks. Arguably, there are as many Mansons outside as inside. Inside, the norm is not Manson nor Willie Horton but the hapless, the invisible, the entirely and thoroughly ordinary. Yet, there is a real and substantial difference between inside and outside. It is a difference in starkness, in the stakes of the games. Inside any jail or prison, life is survival and life-and-death in concrete rather than abstraction. The difference between inside and outside is akin to the difference between a topographical relief map in three dimensions and a flat projection map of the same territory. Both maps can be accurate but the former can be seen and felt more vividly. Inside is that way. Very little is abstract. The availability of a cup of noodles for dinner is life and death, as is the question of whether to walk down a particular corridor or turn a proper corner at some moment.

Criminal law is a relief map of social development. It may be no more accurate and perhaps not nearly as convenient or pricey as flat projections, but it is more exciting on account of high stakes and fast company. Law is a high risk venture.

There are only three standardized examinations for professional entry in the United States: (1) the Graduate Records Examination, (2) the M.C.A.T. for medical school admissions, and (3) the L.S.A.T. for law school. The first two share a basic feature: Both demand memorization as the bulk of the test: What does one recall from four years of undergraduate work? By contrast, the L.S.A.T. asks the Candidate to remember nothing. All the data is provided. Instead of memory, the test demands manipulation of information.

Law and jurisprudence in the United States are argumentative, inherently. The manipulative aspect of law occasions some dismay, even abhorrence, in many, but it remains an essential and fundamental characteristic of the study and profession. Law teaches people how many ways to slice the cheese. By and large, that attorney is more gifted than another who can slice the cheese in more ways. Anyone who can imagine no more than one interpretation of a set of circumstances is a poor candidate or, for that matter, a poor practitioner of the law. By and large, law is fit for those who want the ball when there are only minutes to play and justice is behind on points. There is the excitement. It is there for the taking.

The game metaphor has severe limitations with reference to the law. In fact, the utility of thinking of law as a game is confined by the high stakes involved. Winning and losing are important outcomes, to be sure, but the underlying reality of law is justice, and that never is merely a matter of track record. In criminal trial, prosecution and defense are constrained by truthfulness. In criminal investigations the police are held within the same confines. That individual attorneys and individual police officers have been known to ignore those limits is true but those instances remain idiosyncratic, despite frequency.

Cheap shot artists abound in and about the law. They call attention, for example, to the frequency with which police tell lies. It is true that many officers lie with regularity to everyone or nearly everyone but their own partners. What the cheap shot artist will not bother to mention is that the very nature of policing generates the likelihood that circumstances will arise in which an officer will balance telling a lie against an outcome tacitly understood as a service to society. A prosecutor must be on guard to restrain the zeal of some officers to fabricate testimony in the interests of contributing to a criminal conviction, where the police are certain of the factual guilt of a defendant. Always, it is an error in judgment to imagine that such balancing is either necessary or desirable. Legal guilt must be established within the bounds of absolute allegiance to the truth; only in that manner can legal guilt be reliable, therefore, just. But it ought not to be difficult to understand why some police officers will make the mistake.

Precisely the same is true with regard to officers of the court. Whether the attorney misconstrues the interests of prosecution or defense as sufficiently worthwhile to permit perjury, or misconstrues the attorney's chances of winning the case to permit the same fault, suborning perjury remains inherently opposed to justice because it is opposed to truthfulness. Whether the source of the error be in fee or notoriety and reputation, or in the notion that factual guilt entitles a prosecutor to lie in establishing legal guilt, or defense counsel to lie in order to spare a defendant who may not be innocent legally but who has been victimized by society, it remains an error.

Law demands justice dictated by truth. That is not an individualistic matter nor is it merely a benediction. It is an inherent feature of law as discipline, process and practice. Dictate and demand are absolute masters; they do not become more or less significant or real on account of the frequencies with which they are obeyed or ignored.

Therein lies the challenge of law: It is argumentative and manipulative at the same time as it must function within the confines of truth and justice. Many people will see that simultaneity as a contradiction, reasoning that truth and justice cannot be established by manipulation or argument. That reasoning is profoundly conservative, even reactionary, insisting as it does that perspective can have no place in determining truth and justice. That was the fatal flaw in Platonism: The Athenian nobility, disenfranchised by democracy from their former rule, knew right from wrong with absolute certainty. The sophists who taught rhetoric were regarded as evil-doers on account of their relativism. The reasoning remains as flawed fatally today as in Periclean Greece.

Suum quoque tribuere, to one as to all, is an underlying maxim of distributive justice in the law. It is narrow. It does not specify what it is to which the one may be entitled, merely that, if one is entitled, all must be entitled to the same. The narrowness permits precision and the precision permits absolute allegiance to the principle, a *per se* rule. Balancing has no place in that context. However, understanding the merits or circumstances in a case as a matter which generates the principle certainly is a question of perspective, thus, argument and manipulation of data. For example, does an incarcerated indigent convicted of a felony have a right to first appeal? If the question is answered *suum quoque tribuere*, the answer will be that, if anyone is titled to a first appeal as of right in a jurisdiction, the indigent in that jurisdiction must be as well, thus, appellate fees waived. [*Griffin v. Illinois*] But it is a poor scholar who imagines that the maxim is the only way in which to understand the circumstances of the case. Exactly the same set of circumstances can be seen as a rational-basis test of appellate fees in a particular jurisdiction.

Nemo tenetur seipsum non accusare, not forced against self, is a jurisprudential maxim connected intimately with voluntarism. As such, it is absolute. However, carried to absolute ends it degenerates into *argumentum ad absurdum*, virtually precluding government from prosecuting criminal offenses. Thus, to avoid the absurdity, the maxim begs the question of immunity whereby there can be no compulsion because no liability stemming from incrimination. Immunity, in turn, begs the question of scope, the extent of the immunity coextensive with the scope of the incrimination. That means an argument. Furthermore, the mere suggestion of immunity can become an occasion for heated debate among police and officers of the court. [*Escobedo v. Illinois*]

As the preceding illustrations reveal, the law is at once absolute in principle and argumentative in practice. But the practice cannot violate boundaries established by principles, never, not for any reason(s) whatever. The necessity of understanding perspectives in the law—crime control, due from the dictate of truth and the process, class justice—stems demand for justice.

It is just there, as a perspective, that the political economy developed in this book is important. It is a point of view in which law is seen as rationalization of material productivity and its social organization. In the American experience, the initial jurisprudence of privacy, for example, was based in property law. That jurisprudence developed into the claim that privacy was more fundamental than property; people without property were entitled to privacy nonetheless. But that development has not altered the fact that the zone of privacy remains more or less extensive depending upon wealth, *i.e.*, property. As law demands justice, justice itself is understood according to social institutions developed as indeterminate responses to capital reproduction.

Another illustration of the perspective of political economy lies in considering the jurisprudence of assistance of counsel at trial. From *Powell* through *Argersinger*, the jurisprudence has developed in a context of indigency. Poverty is the sociohistorical and material circumstance which has prompted the legal issue of indigency, and the question of assistance of counsel at trial has never had much significance for the wealthy or even those who were not indigent because they retained counsel as a matter of resources and vested self-interest. Thus, the jurisprudence has developed as a reflection of political economy and its class positioning.

Perhaps the most telling illustration of the central role of political economy in the development of American criminal law is plea bargaining. As the principal means of criminal disposition throughout the United States, plea bargaining accounts for upwards of three-fourths of the caseload. Add to that fact the data on felony indictments throughout the United States, upwards of two-thirds of which are filed against indigents, and it is impossible to escape the inference that most of the guilty pleas entered are from the poor. All the while the United States Supreme Court has upheld the constitutionality of plea bargaining and has generated the ideological disguise according to which, to use one of Chief Justice Rehnquist's signatures, poverty is not a legal issue. Any attempt to appreciate the prevalence and resilience of plea bargaining, not to mention its constitutionality, apart from political economy is doomed. Plea bargaining is class justice *par excellence* in the United States. History generates the truth which, in turn, dictates the demand for justice. People do make their history but not in any way they wish.

History works its way as a channel, carving societies, cultures, and whole civilizations through human behavior. The channeling is generated by some productive force, historically imposed rather than by any overall design or convention. For not less than the past two centuries, throughout the world, that channeling has come as indeterminate response to the formation and reproduction of capital as the fundamental measure of wealth. By "indeterminate," it is understood that socio-historical development works as cause and effect are understood, in the physical and biological sciences, namely, probabilistically rather than deterministically.

Within that channel, some currents become stronger while others eddy. The currents are our social institutions, both overt and abstract. Overt patterns include institutions basic to any society, *e.g.*, family, education, work, medicine, law; the latter emerge from those institutions in the form of ideology or collective belief. Just as institutions develop within limits set by productive forces and class structure, individuality develops in turn within boundaries established by institutions. Manners, fashions and tastes illustrate overt individuality while beliefs and values are abstractions. Individuality, in both overt and abstract forms, emerges and develops as an outcome rather than as a cause of the interplay of social institutions. Wet pavements do not cause rain.

Law amounts to selective mores stated as prohibitions with penalties attached to violations. Where wealth is distributed unequally, as in the United States where less than one-percent of the population effectively controls approximately sixty-five percent of the total wealth, the state develops as an over-arching institution which functions to maintain and stabilize that inequity. To understand law as an arm of the state is to see law as rationalization of the inequitable distribution of wealth. The police power accompanies law as the fist at the end of the arm, at the point of immediate confrontation between law and people.

To reiterate, individuality in both forms of overt behavior and abstract values emerges and develops indeterminately as an outcome of the interplay of institutions. Thus, nothing in the foregoing account of social development suggests conspiracy, oppression, or other pejoratives. There is only history.

The members of a capital-owning class develop indeterminately in consequence of the same generic influences as members of the working class: force and social organization of production. Individuality among capitalists develops indeterminately according to the same generic as does individuality among labor: the interplay of social institutions. The difference between capital and labor as social classes, of course, is found in their distinguishable yet interactive material condition, namely, the former own the means of production while the latter work for wages those means generate. As John Carroll wrote, there are those who own cathedrals and those who clean them. That is the importance of history but it is not inherently oppressive or conspiratorial, Marxists to the contrary notwithstanding.

In the United States, the pattern of social development has been reflected with increasing clarity, drama and inequity, as the number of capital owners has declined while the wealth they control has risen. As Americans regard the dawn of the twenty-first century, they would be well-advised to understand their opportunities and predicaments by centering attention on political economy. That has been the fundamental thesis in this book. It makes no more sense to ignore the historical development of political economy while trying to grasp the reality of social issues than to imagine gun control as though it could be implemented apart from the prevalence of guns.

The criminal justice system in the United States offers a particularly vivid and stark reflection of the more profound issues which are to occupy Americans, whether they realize it, during some substantial portion if not all of the twenty-first century. Criminal justice, as an integrated social system which incorporates all the institutions of law enforcement, criminal law and process, and the prison industry—cops, courts and corrections in the vernacular—reveals a two-tiered, class-structured organization of justice. In each tier, social justice is intertwined with criminal justice and each tier includes both overt and more abstract patterns.

Whether it be the norms of criminal process established by adversarial jurisprudence at trial and the appellate, or norms instituted by the far more frequent process of plea bargaining, those norms reflect nothing any more clearly than the structure of wealth. When the plight of our inner cities and the inhabitants are considered it requires a jaundiced and untrained eye to overlook the fact that political economy is the crux of problems in law enforcement, health, welfare and education. As a perspective, political economy enables us to see as well that these issues of criminal and social justice have become more acute in part because the roots have been hidden in plain view by ideology. This, too, has been historical rather than conspiratorial.

As a metaphor, consider the image of a ship sailing through the Golden Gate. Because the basic structure of ships is part of conventional wisdom it is understood that the portion we see above the water line is buttressed and made possible only within limits set by the foundation of the hull below the water line. But suppose we had no conventional wisdom regarding ships. That is the state of the art with regard to education and political economy. No conspiracy was required because the interplay of institutions in America develop indeterminately into the disguise of classlessness and the costume of individualistic social mobility. No conspiracy was necessary, and attempts would have proven counter-productive in all likelihood, because the best of us were educated to believe that equality was cherished as an ideal and practiced as a virtue. Shortcomings were understood as individualistic breakdowns in an essentially sound process of equitable social development.

All the while, as the fires raged in the inner cities and suburbs and farms became farther removed, as the institution of the American family developed indeterminately in response to industrial and post-industrial wage work, we were able to persuade ourselves that our best had to be enough because it was all we had. The "bottom line" metaphor emerged as a cliche and was taken to mean that entitlement attached to productivity rather than to humanity, *i.e.* you get what you pay for, no free lunch. Generically, the central problem of our society came to be understood as what to do with the unproductive and counter-productive. Criminal justice emerged as one of the central American social systems, whose function was to warehouse a portion of the surplus population generated by the political economy. If repair of criminal justice is to occur, it will be repair of the warehousing function.

Repair lies not in any mysterious or arcane secret buried archaeologically. Rather, we need only notice that we have buried the cause in plain sight. Essentially, it is the significance and workings of political economy, and no more productive and exciting locale in which to begin the repair can be found than law and criminal justice.

But repair inherently involves prescriptions. What is in need of being repaired, how urgently and at what cost? And by whom?

It is necessary to remind one another of the connection between prescription and diagnosis. Where the preliminary stage of the process is erroneous, the latter stage will be ineffective at best and may make conditions worse. The key to intelligent and effective repair lies in diagnosing the criminal justice apparatus for what it does in fact rather than for what we may insist it ought to have been doing. If criminal justice functions in America to screen good people from bad and to punish the bad people in the interests of vengeance or utility, retributive justice or incapacitation, then the current system cries for repair in the form of more frequent and more harsh punishment. But if the empirical reality of criminal justice is a warehousing function, the current system works well, and the questions seem to reduce to more warehouses run more cost-effectively, or a substantial reorganization of the system in order to accomplish something other than warehousing.

The pathway leading criminal justice toward a more punitive paradigm leads through draconian penal codes and enhanced latitude for the police, longer sentences, more prisons and increased frequency of executions. No empirical evidence now exists to falsify such a paradigm because it is futuristic and conditionally scale-oriented, *i.e.*, it calls for more as a solution as yet to be implemented. But it must be observed, on account of the same test of empiricism, that no compelling data exists to show that a more punitive criminal justice will succeed.

The closing several decades of the twentieth century in the United States have witnessed increasing incarceration as the emergent criminal justice policy. However, the policy has developed amidst increasing rates of crimes reported to police and arrests and prosecutions leading to convictions. In short, greatly enhanced rates and lengths of incarceration have yet to reduce crime significantly. While it has been argued that more resources poured into developing a more punitive criminal justice will succeed, it has not happened yet. Empirically, the inference that we should increase support for a more punitive system is no more compelling than the notion that we ought to cut our losses and turn to something very different.

One image of American criminal justice in the twenty-first century which emerges is that of a garrison society, *i.e.*, social organization in which about the same percent of the whole population are engaged, directly or indirectly, in custodial supervision as the number of those incarcerated. While such an image runs counter to conventional American ideology, history has seen impressive displays of the adaptabability and resilience of ideology. After all, ideology follows political economy rather than the other way around. Still, the garrison state is a bleak and uninspiring landscape.

Seen from the perspective of political economy, the acid test of policy and direction in America has been and remains cost-effectiveness. No more clear demonstration of the dominance and consistency of that test can be had than criminal justice. The image of police officers as crime-fighters which has become paradigmatic, of activist courts implementing what had to be implemented and of the prison industry developing as a smaller-scale-more-cost-effective big house, all developed historically in the United States as indeterminate outcomes of allegiance to cost-effectiveness.

When cost-effectiveness is used as the test of future directions in criminal justice, one thing becomes clear immediately: Incarceration alone is a prophecy for disaster simply because it costs too much. That begs the question of whether it is possible to reduce costs while enhancing the utility of incarceration. Logically, one response is to reduce costs by decreasing the length of incarceration through increased use of capital punishment. Would it be possible to lower the average cost of execution if executions were done on volume? Advocates of draconian punishment might be taken at their word, and the indices permitting the use of such punishment expanded to somewhere near the eighteenth-century level when, under English law, there were more than two hundred capital offenses and men were hanged for steeling sheep. For all those chilled by such a prospect, there might be an equal number who would look forward to it. Besides, ideological obstacles might be overcome by the benefits of increasing cost-effectiveness, and not for the first time in American history.

Is there nothing on the horizon any more appealing than increasingly draconian measures in one form or another? Is there no realistic hope of developing criminal justice toward more humane and productive ends than either vengeance or incarceration seem to offer?

In approaching these questions it is essential to realize that ideology is formed in service to capital formation and as indeterminate outcome of the interplay of institutionalized patterns, which developed themselves as rationalization for capital. Therefore, future directions are not to be considered accurately as though the process of development involved nothing more fundamental than logic. A people does not, willy-nilly, shift from one paradigm to another, or do so by convention and design. What is required for such a shift is a persuasive praxis over time which demonstrates convincingly that the force of production will benefit more significantly from realignment and reorganization than from development in the direction marked by the status quo. Such praxis means struggle, and a great deal of it. If such realignment is possible, it can not be done easily or conveniently.

There are those who insist that thinking never solved anything, that what is required to redirect criminal justice is not thought but action. Political economy teaches that thought is human action. From this perspective, one of the weaknesses in traditional Anglo-American jurisprudence lies in the dichotomy posed between thought and action, between thought and behavior. Thought is human behavior, not all of it or all forms of it, to be sure, but nothing is more intricately a dimension of human behavior than thought.

Thus, the praxis required for an effective realignment of criminal justice away from warehousing surplus peoples, away from retribution and cost-begging use of incarceration, requires rethinking the system fundamentally: Other than warehousing, what might a criminal justice system in the United States accomplish? Is it inherent in criminal justice that the institution remain a cost to capital formation and development, or might the system be rearranged basically as a benefit? Vengeance or retributive justice seem counter-productive in cost/benefit terms, but what utilitarian value beyond mere incapacitation can be had through a criminal justice system? If law inherently involves social control, can that control be affected in the United States in the twenty-first century in ways which are both more cost-effective and more humane than our current system?

Once again, historical truth has dictated the questions. Once again, history waits to find what justice will demand.

Dicta

Three Families

There was the afternoon in the dining room of the *Sol Mar,* the elegant Mexican rancho situated on one of the loveliest spots on earth, the absolute tip of Baja where the Pacific and the Sea of Cortez run together. It was the middle of August, when Cabo San Lucas becomes a favorite place in which to escape the summer heat. At each of the two tables, a Mexican family took their principal meal of the day.

At one of these tables sat grandfather, father and son. They were dressed casually in loose-fitting white linen. They spoke only in Spanish or, more accurately, the Mexican version thereof. At the other table were grandfather, father, mother and son, each of whom was comfortable while speaking now in Spanish, now in French and, when it was Spanish, it was Castilian rather than Mexican. Two Mexican families; one of the upper middle class, the other, patrician.

It is a thing one can see in Mexico, this delicate blend of mingling and distance. Each of the families was wealthy; in each, females as well as males were privileged by formal education. In each family, the son was seventeen or eighteen, healthy, good-looking, confident and at ease. Luis was enjoying summer vacation from his studies at the university in Mexico City; Miguel was home for the summer from school in France. Luis was pre-med; Miguel was reading philosophy. Luis's thick black hair blended with his swarthy complexion while Miguel's sandy hair and skin showed the tanning effects of the summer sun. Luis and Miguel sat at separate tables in a fine dining room. Each was occupied with his own thoughts and the interaction with his family. In the years to come it was to be that Luis would continue to develop the family's fortunes as a respected physician who would enter politics with a seat in the cabinet of two presidents. Miguel would please his family by keeping his name, and that of his future bride, out of the newspapers and, throughout his long and pleasant life, it would never occur to him to wonder about what it was he did or how he spent his time. Neither Luis nor Miguel would ever know poverty but having money would be a comforting category in which to think about the world for Luis while, for Miguel, money would never be anything to think about at all.

The fisherman who had brought in the catch which the two wealthy families consumed that afternoon was named Lupe, and he was a person of long life and experience and skill in the waters south of La Paz along the coast of Baja. As a younger man, Lupe had fished the waters off Espiritu Santo and had fought sharks for a catch but now, with his sons and daughters, he lived in a shack near the water just beyond the old cannery in Cabo. Lupe's house had a floor of dirt, an assortment of corrugated and planed scraps for walls, and a roof of thatched palm which kept out a certain amount of heat without blocking any of the breeze which cooled the cape. Two roosters and an uncounted number of hens had the run of the place, along with Lupe's four younger children. Lupe and his wife had been blessed as well with two older sons and three daughters. Of these, one daughter had died in infancy, one had a job as a maid at the *Finisterra,* and the other daughter the family does not speak of; each of the sons is married, one lives up the coast in Santo Rosario and the other older son, together with his wife and two young children, live with Lupe and his wife. This son helps his father with the fishing.

It had never seemed to Lupe that there were too many people or too little room. He leaves his house before the sun appears and, in the evening when he returns after selling his catch at one of the hotels, it is pleasant to sit and watch the young ones and make plans with his son to fish the next day.

Lupe has no ambition. He has industry, but no ambition. Once, about eight years before, Lupe had an ambition and, for three years, every member of the family who was able to earn a single peso which did not have to be spent for living contributed to a sum which Lupe's wife cared for and which, when it had grown large enough, went for the purchase of a second-hand but very fine motor engine which Lupe hung on the stern of his old skiff. So, for the past five years or so, Lupe has enjoyed the luxury of being able to use his patched sail or, whenever he has wished as long as there was some gasoline, to use his outboard.

Lupe knows that, if he absolutely had to, he could run his skiff out into the Pacific, though he does not do so regularly because the waters there are so much harder on the old boat. Some day, the engine will belong to Lupe's son.

Suggestions for Additional Reading

Part One. The Structure of Case Law and Perspectives on American Criminal Jurisprudence

John Steinbeck, *The Log from the Sea of Cortez*, [Viking: 1951]

Packer, Herbert, *The Limits of the Criminal Sanction*, [Stanford University Press: 1968]

Miller, Stuart Creighton, *The Unwelcome Immigrant: the American Image of the Chinese, 1786–1882,* [University of California Press: 1969]

Charles A. & Mary R. Beard, *The Rise of American Civilization*, [Macmillan: 1930]

Max Lerner, *America as a Civilization: Life and Thought in the United States Today,* [Simon and Schuster: 1957]

Schwartz, Bernard, *A History of the Supreme Court,* [Oxford University Press: 1993]

Kermit L. Hall (ed.), *The Oxford Companion to the Supreme Court of the United States,* [Oxford University Press: 1992]

K. N. Llewellyn, *The Bramble Bush: On Our Law and Its Study,* [Oceana Publications: 1930, 1960]

Part Two. Law Enforcement and the Courts on Search and Seizure

Harriet Ziskin, *The Blind Eagle: Stories from the Courtroom,* [Early Stages Press: 1982]

G. William Domhoff, *Who Rules America?* [Prentice-Hall: 1967]

Jeffrey H. Reiman, *The Rich Get Richer and the Poor Get Prison,* Fourth Edition, [John Wiley & Sons: 1994]

Raymond Williams, *Problems in Materialism and Culture: Selected Essays,* [Verso: 1980]

Barton J. Bernstein (ed.), *Towards a New Past: Dissenting Essays in American History,* [Vintage Books/Random House: 1969]

Elliot Liebow, *Tally's Corner: A Study of Negro Streetcorner Men,* [Little, Brown: 1967]

Bruce Catton, *The Civil War,* [Fairfax Press: 1980]

Part Three. Voluntarism and Counsel: The Fifth and Sixth Amendments

Haywood Patterson, *Scottsboro Boy,* [Doubleday: 1952]

Anthony Lewis, *Gideon's Trumpet*

Piers Beirne & Richard Quinney (eds.), *Marxism and Law,* [John Wiley & Sons: 1982]

Edgar Dunn, *Economic and Social Development: A Process of Social Learning,* [Johns Hopkins Press: 1971]

Jonathan Kozol, *Illiterate America,* [Anchor Press/Doubleday: 1985]

Stephen Steinberg, *The Ethnic Myth: Race, Ethnicity, and Class in America,* [Beacon Press: 1989]

Gabriel Kolko, *Wealth and Power in America: An Analysis of Social Class and Income Distribution,* [Praeger: 1962]

David F. Greenberg (ed.), *Crime and Capitalism: Readings in Marxist Criminology,* [Mayfield: 1981]

Glossary

U.S. Constitution Amendments Four, Five, Six, Eight	Provisions within the Bill of Rights which established the constitutional framework within which American constitutional criminal jurisprudence has developed as restraint against rather than enhancement of the power of government to obtain criminal convictions.
antinomy	A contradiction, as in Packer's "normative antinomy" as contradictory values.
Fourth Amendment	prohibition against "unreasonable searches and seizure" guarantees of warrant, probable cause and the exclusionary rule
Fifth Amendment	prohibition against double jeopardy guarantees of due process
Sixth Amendment	guarantees of assistance of counsel and jury trial
Eighth Amendment	prohibition against "cruel and unusual punishment"
appellate	1. a court, whether state or federal, in which the primary concern is the possibility of legal error on the part of a court of prior jurisdiction in a given case; 2. a process by which to petition for review of a criminal conviction.
arm of the state	Used in political economy to refer to law generically as rationalization of the state.
Bill of Rights	Ratified 1791 as the first ten amendments to the U.S. Constitution, these provisions attached to the central government exclusively as restraints on the legitimate use of power.
brief	A condensation or abstract of an original case, as in a summary of a case according to issue, reasoning, application and conclusion (IRAC) prepared by a law student.

certiorari — A court order from an appellate court to a court of prior jurisdiction to submit all materials of a case.

ceterus paribus — all other being equal

Civil War Amendments — Amendments Thirteen (1865), Fourteen (1868) and Fifteen (1870) ratified as parts of the U.S. Constitution as an indirect and immediate result of the Civil War, 1861–1865; these amendments were proposed and ratified as constitutional guarantees against secessionist issues being raised in the future.

common law

1. law established, maintained and changed case-by-case;
2. judge-made law;
3. the title of a classic book by Oliver Wendell Holmes.

confederation — A structure for government in which the major powers reside in the separate units rather than in the central unit, *e.g.*, Articles of Confederation, the Confederate States America.

convergence

1. to come together; to merge;
2. jurisprudential theory that distinctive sections of the U.S. Constitution, for all their distinguishability, generate a single jurisprudence in the light of a set of circumstances;
3. in relation to the Fourth and Fifth Amendments and the privacy penumbra, see *Boyd v. U.S.*;
4. in relation to the Fifth and Sixth Amendments and the implication of voluntarism, see *Escobedo v. Illinois* and *Miranda v. Arizona*;
5. *e.g.*, any of the First Amendment guarantees might be held to reach the same implication as the privacy penumbra found in the Fourth and Fifth Amendments; see argument before the U.S. District Court as trier-of-fact in *Roe v. Wade*.

crime control — A normative model developed by Herbert Packer in which American criminal process is to be understood as developing according to the efficiency of informal, non-adjudicative screening of suspects by police and prosecutors.

determinism	1. the doctrine of cause understood as antecedent stimulus producing consequent reaction 2. the tacit view that cause itself can not be understood except as A causes B, *i.e.*, everytime A, then B. 3. an attack drawn from conventional reasoning in which political economy is branded as single-factor reduction and dogma.
duces tecum	To bring with; a subpoena from a court to insure that a person appearing in a particular matter will be in possession and surrender to court use of materials essential to adjudication.
due process	1. explicit phrase found in the Fifth and Fourteenth Amendments, U.S. Constitution; 2. guarantees, whether explicit or implicit, essential to the Bill of Rights and/or "the concept of ordered liberty;" 3. a normative model of criminal process in the U.S. developed by Herbert Packer according to which the subject is understood as development according to the values of reliability and equality, maintained by erecting obstacles of formal adjudication in the path of government power to secure criminal convictions.
Due Process Clause, Amendment Fourteen, U.S. Constitution	Attached explicitly as generic restraint against the power of states but without any explication of specific restraints to be understood as included, thereby begging development of incorporation.
empirical	1. factual, intersubjectively testable information in science; 2. objective data in comparison to normative information; 3. information aimed at description and explanation rather than at prescription or advocacy.
et al	and all the others
etcetera (etc.)	and so forth
ex vi termini	without exception

federation	A structure for government in which the major powers reside in the central unit, although significant powers may be shared between the central unit and the satellite units and other powers may reside exclusively in the satellite units, *e.g.*, the United States of America.
folkways	According to William Graham Sumner, these are the relatively unimportant or innocuous norms of a society.
habeas corpus	1. to present the body; 2. to protest the conditions of confinement; 3. a court order to an agent of government to see that a petitioner is brought before a court at a day and time for a hearing; 4. a major concern of the Rehnquist court in its desire to reduce the appellate caseload of the federal judiciary.
the hegemonic	1. explicated originally in the Prison Notebooks of Antonio Gramsci; 2. according to Raymond Williams, the term refers to the most basic order or sense of meaning and value in the minds of the overwhelming members of a society; the way they understand the world in the most fundamental terms; 3. according to Williams, distinct from ideology because more deeply and less consciously understood; according to conventional sociology, a form of ideology.
ideology	1. conventionally, the collective values and beliefs of a whole people which function as an important source or direction for their behavior; 2. in political economy, an institutionalized set of abstractions available for study and developed indeterminately as rationalization of the more overt institutions; 3. Marx referred to it as a disguise, and Daniel Bell as a Coney Island mirror, meaning that ideology does reflect the collective wisdom of a people but in a manner distorted by the nature of ideology as rationalization for the political economy.

ideographic
1. information of an individualistic nature, not likely to be repeated exactly;
2. one-shot data; unique information;
3. in set theory, information about one or more members of a set rather than about the set *per se*

incorporation
1. In constitutional law, the issue of what specific restraints are attached to the states by virtue of the Fourteenth Amendment Due Process Clause.
2. the argument between *in toto* and selective process.

in toto incorporation
1. The answer to the incorporation question according to which the Fourteenth Amendment Due Process Clause refers to all and only those specific restraints made explicit in the Bill of Rights
2. advocated consistently only by Associate Justice Hugo Lafayette Black and most clearly explicated in Justice Black's dissent in *Adamson v. California.*

selective incorporation
1. substantive due process;
2. The answer to the incorporation question according to which "the concept of ordered liberty" has been the exclusive jurisprudential formula for determining which precise guarantees, whether explicitly or implicitly found in the U.S. Constitution, are to be included within the meaning of due process in the Fourteenth Amendment, thus, attached in restraint against the states;
3. most clearly explicated by Justice Cardozo in *Palko v. Connecticut.*

indeterminacy
1. in physics, the notion of responses which cannot be fixed except within an order of probability established by the discernible cause;
2. in philosophy, the view that, while human behavior always occurs within historically-imposed circumstances, it develops with considerable latitude;
3. in political economy, the image of cause as a force which generates limits to development, *i.e.,* some outcomes are possible, others impossible, and within which limits, some outcomes are more likely, others less, *e.g.*, institutions as socially organized outcomes

of the force and class structure of productivity, and individuality emerges as a further outcome within limits set proximately by institutions.

i.e. — in other words

I.R.A.C. — law school jargon for issue, reasoning, application, and conclusion as the basic outline of any case

jurisprudence
1. the science or philosophy of law; the basis for ascertaining particular applications in law; principles, underlying rules;
2. in a legal argument, jurisprudence will provide the more profound and broad base of reasoning for more limited applications peculiar to a case at hand;
3. in a brief, reasoning related to yet distinguishable from application.

law
1. according to Sumner, prohibitions drawn from the mores of a society; social control;
2. in political economy, prohibitions made necessary in institutional form as rationalization for the organization of a society generated by its productive force(s);
3. an arm of the state, in Marxist context.

mandamus — A court order to an agent of government to carry out the duties of office, *e.g.*, *Marbury v. Madison.*

mode of production — A Marxist metaphor referring to a synthesis of the basic force of production and the class structure that force generates as social relations.

mores
1. According to Sumner, the significant norms of a society, distinguishable from the more innocuous folkways;
2. G. B. Shaw once distinguished caustically between "churchgoing" in America and religiosity, implying that the former was one of the mores while the latter was a mere folkway;
3. the source of law as prohibitions; those particular mores to be enforced by the organized and legitimate use of coercive force in society.

nemo tenetur seibum non accusare
1. not against the self;
2. the jurisprudential formula for the Fifth Amendment prohibition against compulsory self-incrimination;
3. a major part of the "zone of Privacy" jurisprudence in the merger of the Fourth and Fifth Amendments, see *Boyd v. U.S.*
4. an important aspect of the doctrine of voluntarism in American constitutional criminal procedure, according to which behavior is reliable only when it has not been coerced;
5. an important aspect of the argument against the admissibility of confessions (see A.C.L.U. *amicus* brief in *Miranda*) and guilty pleas, thus, plea bargaining.

nomothetic
1. information in pattern, as a pattern, *e.g.*, a social institution;
2. a motif or recurrent theme;
3. in set theory, information about a set rather than about one or more members of a set.
4. empirical models and studies will be rooted in the nomothetic data whereas people conventionally will take it for granted that all information is ideographic, as in normative data.

normative — value-laden, dealing with belief, opinion, ideology

nota bene (N.B.) — to take notice; to note well

penumbra — implied power; implications found in the explicit provisions of the Bill of Rights or elsewhere in the U.S. Constitution, *e.g.*, privacy, abortion, the exclusionary rule; penumbras (plural); penumbrially (adverbial).

per curiam — by the court

per se — of or in itself

pro se — by oneself, as in a defendant as his own counsel

perspectives — crystallizations via social process of basic views; climates of opinion; paradigms; *e.g.*, crime control, due process, class justice

precedent	an antecedent case cited as authority for a subsequent holding
probable cause	When an arresting officer's direct information would provide a reasonable person of prudent caution with the belief that a criminal offense was or was about to be committed; see *Brinegar v. U. S.*
produktionsgeschicte	1. the study of productivity in a society; 2. how productivity is generated and society organized toward that end; 3. a biosocial image of the social organization of organisms in population as indeterminate response to the factor(s) generating reproduction, whether at the evobiological or sociohistorical level; 4. the study of the ultimate source of people's understanding in a society according to the manner in which they are organized by historical force(s) to reproduce themselves in particular ways.
reasonable, articulable suspicion	1. a jurisprudential measure for determining whether police had a reasonable basis for intervening in the behavior of citizens; 2. whether the police officer can explain what he/she noticed which created suspicion of criminal activity; 3. a less demanding standard than probable cause, and often a prior condition of probable cause, as in *Terry v. Ohio*; 4. courts will apply a "totality of circumstances" rather than a *per se* test in measuring reasonable suspicion.
reasonable man doctrine	1. developed as case law in *Brinegar v. U.S.* 2. this abstraction has developed as the jurisprudential formula for determining reasonableness in a Fourth Amendment context; 3. the formula asks whether, in the circumstances before the court, a hypothetical person of prudence and caution would have arrived at the same inference the police drew from those circumstances.
selective incorporation	see incorporation

silver platter doctrine	An implication found in *Weeks v. U.S.* according to which all that was necessary in order to use evidence in federal court which had been contaminated by the unconstitutional manner in which it had been gathered in violation of the Fourth Amendment was to see to it that state or local officers rather than federal officers had done the gathering.
stare decisis	to abide by, as in citing cases as precedents
social institution(s)	1. patterns of behavior engaged in by substantial numbers of the members of a society; 2. conventionally, the results of values, beliefs and conscious choice, at individualistic and pluralistic levels; 3. in political economy, the indeterminate results of the mode of production, and the proximate source of ideology in a society; 4. historical impositions.
the state	1. conventionally, government itself or a state within the United States; 2. *status quo*, as in the state of affairs or the state of the art; 3. in political economy, the inequitable distribution of wealth in a society, as in, law as arm of the state.
suppress (motion to suppress)	A pre-trial attempt, usually by the defense in criminal procedure, to prevent information or other material from coming to the attention of judge and/or jury as evidence during trial.
suum quoque tribuere	1. to one as to all; 2. the jurisprudential formula for fairness; 3. the jurisprudential meaning of due process; 4. the measure does not specify what it is to which the one may be entitled, only that if one is entitled, all must be entitled.
in toto	see incorporation
toto coelo	difference in kind rather than degree
totality of circumstance	a balancing rather than *per se* test of reasonableness

trier-of-fact	A court of original jurisdiction, whether local, state or federal, where the primary consideration is given to determining by formal adjudication and evidentiary norms the legal guilt or innocence of the accused.
usus loquendi	meaning as spoken; usage determines meaning
viz	namely
writ	a court order